Learning JavaScript Robotics

Design, build, and program your own remarkable
robots with JavaScript and open source hardware

Kassandra Perch

BIRMINGHAM - MUMBAI

Learning JavaScript Robotics

First published: November 2015

Production reference: 1231115

Published by Packt Publishing Ltd.
Livery Place
35 Livery Street
Birmingham B3 2PB, UK.

ISBN 978-1-78588-334-7

www.packtpub.com

Credits

Author
Kassandra Perch

Reviewers
Chris S. Crawford
Tomomi Imura

Commissioning Editor
Neil Alexander

Acquisition Editor
Aaron Lazar

Content Development Editor
Mayur Pawanikar

Technical Editor
Menza Mathew

Copy Editor
Kausambhi Majumdar

Project Coordinator
Nidhi Joshi

Proofreader
Safis Editing

Indexer
Rekha Nair

Production Coordinator
Manu Joseph

Cover Work
Manu Joseph

About the Author

Kassandra Perch is an open web developer and supporter. She began as a frontend developer and moved to server-side with the advent of Node.js and was especially enthralled by the advance of the NodeBots community. She travels the world speaking at conferences about NodeBots and the fantastic community around them. When she's not building bots, she's knitting, sewing, sculpting, or playing video games with her cats.

I'd like to thank my mentor—as I've said in the past, I don't know where I'd be without you, but I certainly know my life is better with you in it. My parents supported me as a child who took things apart, and their support lets me continue to do so, as well as build things of my own.

The NodeBots community deserves a huge thank you: your sense of wonder and joy in learning new things keeps me going. Special thanks to Rick and Raquel for getting me started.

About the Reviewers

Chris S. Crawford (@chris_crawford_) is a PhD student in Human-Centered Computing at the University of Florida. He is currently a graduate researcher in Brain-Computer Interface Research Group in Human-Experience Research Lab. His research focus is Brain-Robot Interaction, which consists of investigating the ways in which physiological signals such as electroencephalogram (EEG) can be used to enhance human-robot interactions. Chris has experience of working in various areas including perceptual computing, 3D computer graphics, televoting, and native/web app development. Currently, he also serves as a lead software engineer for SeniorGeek Communications, LLC.

Tomomi Imura (@girlie_mac) is an avid open web and open technology advocate, a frontend engineer, and a creative technologist, who has been active in the mobile space for more than 8 years, before she started working with Internet of Things. She loves to hack with hardware and occasionally gives talks at conferences and workshops on prototyping IoT with Raspberry Pi.

She works as a senior developer evangelist at the San Francisco-based data stream provider, PubNub, to support the best developer experiences.

www.PacktPub.com

Support files, eBooks, discount offers, and more

For support files and downloads related to your book, please visit www.PacktPub.com.

Did you know that Packt offers eBook versions of every book published, with PDF and ePub files available? You can upgrade to the eBook version at www.PacktPub.com and as a print book customer, you are entitled to a discount on the eBook copy. Get in touch with us at service@packtpub.com for more details.

At www.PacktPub.com, you can also read a collection of free technical articles, sign up for a range of free newsletters and receive exclusive discounts and offers on Packt books and eBooks.

https://www2.packtpub.com/books/subscription/packtlib

Do you need instant solutions to your IT questions? PacktLib is Packt's online digital book library. Here, you can search, access, and read Packt's entire library of books.

Why subscribe?

- Fully searchable across every book published by Packt
- Copy and paste, print, and bookmark content
- On demand and accessible via a web browser

Free access for Packt account holders

If you have an account with Packt atwww.PacktPub.com, you can use this to access PacktLib today and view 9entirely free books. Simply use your login credentials for immediate access.

Table of Contents

Preface

Hello! Welcome to *Learning JavaScript Robotics*. In this book, you'll learn how to write code for Arduino and other robotics platforms in JavaScript using Johnny-Five. We'll cover the basics of Johnny-Five, input and output devices, and even movement devices such as servos and motors. Finally, we'll cover how to connect your bots to the Internet and move your Johnny-Five code between different platforms.

What this book covers

Chapter 1, Getting Started with JS Robotics, will get you started by setting up an Arduino Uno and exploring the world of NodeBots.

Chapter 2, Working with Johnny-Five, covers the basics of Johnny-Five, including Read-Eval-Print-Loop (REPL), and we will build our first project.

Chapter 3, Using Digital and PWM Output Pins, covers basic output devices, using both digital and PWM pins.

Chapter 4, Using Specialized Output Devices, covers specialized outputs that use one or multiple pins.

Chapter 5, Using Input Devices and Sensors, covers input devices using analog and GPIO pins.

Chapter 6, Moving Your Bot, covers basic servo and motor usage with Johnny-Five.

Chapter 7, Advanced Movement with the Animation Library, covers the Animation Library and how to create advanced movement schemes for your NodeBots.

Chapter 8, Advanced Components – SPI, I2C, and Other Devices, covers the use of I2C, SPI, and other advanced components with Johnny-Five.

Chapter 9, Connecting NodeBots to the World, and Where to Go Next, covers how to connect your NodeBots to the Internet and use Johnny-Five code with platforms other than Arduino.

What you need for this book

You will need the following factors before you start working on the book:

- A basic working knowledge of JavaScript and Node.JS
- A computer with USB ports that supports node-serialport, running Node.JS 4.x
- An Arduino Uno or other board supported by Johnny-Five (see `http://johnny-five.io/platform-support`) and a USB cable for the board
- Light-Emitting Diodes (LEDs) - having a dozen should let you finish all the examples with room for error.
- A Piezo element
- A character LCD (one with an I2C interface is fine)
- A push-button that is breadboard friendly
- A rotating potentiometer that is breadboard friendly
- A light-sensing diode
- A basic temperature sensor
- Three hobby servos that runs on 5V
- One hobby motor that runs on 5v
- An ADXL345I2C Accelerometer
- An LED matrix kit from SparkFun—product number DEV-11861
- A GamePad—RetroLink N64 controller or a DualShock3
- (Optional) A Particle Photon microcontroller

Who this book is for

If you've worked with Arduino before or are new to electronics and would like to try writing sketches in JavaScript, then this book is for you. A basic knowledge of JavaScript and Node.js will help you get the most out of this book.

Conventions

In this book, you will find a number of text styles that distinguish between different kinds of information. Here are some examples of these styles and an explanation of their meaning.

Code words in text, database table names, folder names, filenames, file extensions, pathnames, dummy URLs, user input, and Twitter handles are shown as follows: "For instance, the LED object has an on() and off() function that turns the LED on and off."

A block of code is set as follows:

```
var myPin = new five.Pin(11);
myPin.on('high', function(){
console.log('pin 11 set to high!');
});
```

When we wish to draw your attention to a particular part of a code block, the relevant lines or items are set in bold:

```
var myPin = new five.Pin(11);
myPin.on('high', function(){
console.log('pin 11 set to high!');
});
```

Any command-line input or output is written as follows:

```
> node LED-repl.js
```

New terms and **important words** are shown in bold. Words that you see on the screen, for example, in menus or dialog boxes, appear in the text like this: "Now, we'll build a couple of projects that demonstrate how to use more advanced sensors: a **photocell** and a **temperature** sensor."

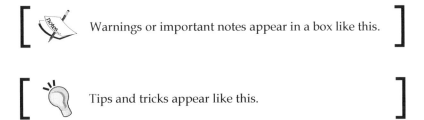

Warnings or important notes appear in a box like this.

Tips and tricks appear like this.

Reader feedback

Feedback from our readers is always welcome. Let us know what you think about this book—what you liked or disliked. Reader feedback is important for us as it helps us develop titles that you will really get the most out of.

To send us general feedback, simply e-mail feedback@packtpub.com, and mention the book's title in the subject of your message.

If there is a topic that you have expertise in and you are interested in either writing or contributing to a book, see our author guide at www.packtpub.com/authors.

Customer support

Now that you are the proud owner of a Packt book, we have a number of things to help you to get the most from your purchase.

Downloading the example code

You can download the example code files from your account at http://www.packtpub.com for all the Packt Publishing books you have purchased. If you purchased this book elsewhere, you can visit http://www.packtpub.com/support and register to have the files e-mailed directly to you.

Downloading the color images of this book

We also provide you with a PDF file that has color images of the screenshots/diagrams used in this book. The color images will help you better understand the changes in the output. You can download this file from: https://www.packtpub.com/sites/default/files/downloads/3347OS_ColoredImages.pdf.

Errata

Although we have taken every care to ensure the accuracy of our content, mistakes do happen. If you find a mistake in one of our books—maybe a mistake in the text or the code—we would be grateful if you could report this to us. By doing so, you can save other readers from frustration and help us improve subsequent versions of this book. If you find any errata, please report them by visiting http://www.packtpub.com/submit-errata, selecting your book, clicking on the **Errata Submission Form** link, and entering the details of your errata. Once your errata are verified, your submission will be accepted and the errata will be uploaded to our website or added to any list of existing errata under the Errata section of that title.

To view the previously submitted errata, go to https://www.packtpub.com/books/content/support and enter the name of the book in the search field. The required information will appear under the **Errata** section.

Piracy

Piracy of copyrighted material on the Internet is an ongoing problem across all media. At Packt, we take the protection of our copyright and licenses very seriously. If you come across any illegal copies of our works in any form on the Internet, please provide us with the location address or website name immediately so that we can pursue a remedy.

Please contact us at copyright@packtpub.com with a link to the suspected pirated material.

We appreciate your help in protecting our authors and our ability to bring you valuable content.

Questions

If you have a problem with any aspect of this book, you can contact us at questions@packtpub.com, and we will do our best to address the problem.

1
Getting Started with JS Robotics

Welcome to the world of JavaScript robotics! Let's explore how easy it is to get started with writing robotics programs in JavaScript using Arduino and Johnny-Five.

In this chapter, we will do the following:

- Explore JS Robotics, NodeBots, and Johnny-Five
- Set up our development environment
- Blink an on-board LED

Understanding JS Robotics, NodeBots, and Johnny-Five

JavaScript as a robotics language truly began a few years ago with the creation of **node-serialport**—an NPM module written by Chris Williams. This module allows Node.JS to communicate with devices over a serial connection; this can include the typical serial connections from older computers, or the USB and Bluetooth connections that we use every day. What exactly is a **NodeBot** though, and how do we get started with using them with Johnny-Five?

What a NodeBot is, and other basic vocabulary

A NodeBot is any piece of hardware that is controlled using JavaScript and/or Node. JS. This can encompass a wide variety of projects; there are hundreds of ways to create a NodeBot. In this book, we are going to use the Johnny-Five library, an open source project created by Rick Waldron.

 For those readers who are new to robotics, a microcontroller is a small computer that contains a processor, memory, and input/output pins. This serves as the brain of our project—our programs will communicate with or will be loaded onto this microcontroller. Microcontrollers come in many shapes and sizes, and with multiple capabilities.

We're going to use a microcontroller for our projects. What microcontroller should you use? Luckily, our use of Johnny-Five means that we can choose from a large array of different microcontrollers and *still write the same code as you'll see in this book!*

What exactly is Johnny-Five, and how does it make our lives easier?

Johnny-Five and the NodeBot revolution

Johnny-Five (`https://johnny-five.io`) is an open source robotics library for Node.JS. It was created by Rick Waldron and has a thriving community of contributors and supporters. This module has been known to work on Windows, Mac, and Linux computers without any issues at the time of writing this book using Node.JS version 4.x.

Johnny-Five was built on top of node-serialport and allows us to write JavaScript applications that communicate with different microcontrollers using different types of connection. For some microcontrollers, such as Arduino-compatible boards, Johnny-Five uses a serial connection. For some newer boards, Johnny-Five emulates this serial connection over an Internet service!

The capability of Johnny-Five to use multiple board types is implemented using its wrapper system. Once the core system is installed, you can install a wrapper for your particular microcontroller, and the APIs will remain the same. This is a powerful concept—you can write code for one platform and quickly move it to another without having to change it.

What we'll be using in this book

For the examples in this book, we'll use an Arduino Uno board. You can get these boards from sites such as Adafruit (www.adafruit.com), SparkFun (www.sparkfun.com), and so on. You can also use a board that is Arduino Uno-compatible. SainSmart, for instance, sells Uno-like boards that will work fine for our purposes. For this chapter, you'll need the board itself and a USB cable for it.

In later chapters, we'll be using other components—there will be a table in each chapter with an accessible list of materials for the projects within.

Setting up your development environment

Now that we've covered the basic ideas, we're going to set up the development environment for our first project. All the software used here worked on Windows, Mac, and Linux desktop computers at the time of writing this book.

Installing Node.JS

If you don't have Node.JS already installed, you can download an installer for your platform from nodejs.org. This installer will also install **NPM** or **Node Package Manager**, which will be used to manage the rest of the software that we'll be using.

Run the installer on your machine, which may require a restart. After this, open up your terminal application and run the following command:

```
node --version
```

The output from this command should be 4.x.x, where x are integers.

Setting up your project and installing Johnny-Five

In your terminal, create a folder for your project and change directories to this folder:

```
mkdir my-robotics-project
cd my-robotics-project
```

Next, we're going to install Johnny-Five:

```
npm install johnny-five
```

You should see a spinner, followed by some output. Unless you see an **ERR NOT OK** message at the end of your output, you're good to go with Johnny-Five.

 On a Mac machine, you may need to install XCode developer command-line tools.

Connecting your Microcontroller and installing Firmata

First, you should get the Arduino IDE. Yes, we are still using JavaScript; however, we must make sure that there's a particular sketch (that's Arduino-speak for program) running on our board in order for Johnny-Five to communicate properly.

You can get the installer at the Arduino website (`http://www.arduino.cc/en/Main/Software`). This book assumes that you have version 1.6.4, but the versions in the 1.4 range should work as well.

Once you've downloaded the software, open it. Then, we'll make sure that your serial connection works.

 If you are using a board other than an Arduino, this step is not necessary. However, there may be other steps. These will be outlined with the wrapper plugin for your board.

Plug the USB cable into both the board and the computer. A few LEDs should light up on this board—this is normal. Then, go to the **Tools** menu in the Arduino IDE and hover over the **ports** submenu. You should see a list of ports that looks somewhat like the following screenshot:

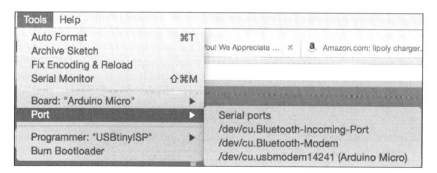

You should see at least one entry in this list that fits the following format: **/dev/ cu.usbmodem*******. It may or may not have **Arduino Uno** next to it. If you see this, go ahead and click on it, because this is the port you will want to use for the Firmata installation. If you have this, it means your board can communicate with your computer, and you're ready to install Firmata.

To install Firmata on your board, go to **File | Examples | Firmata | StandardFirmata**, as shown in the following screenshot:

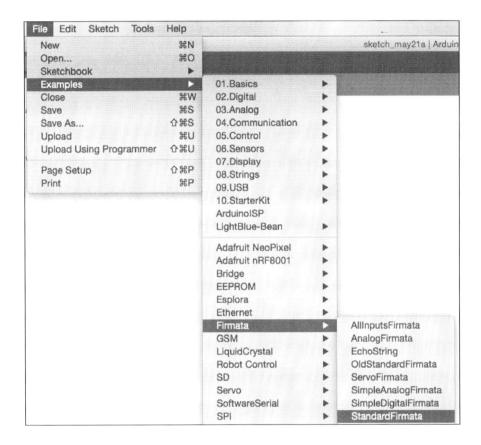

Once you've opened the sketch, you should get an IDE window that looks like the following screenshot:

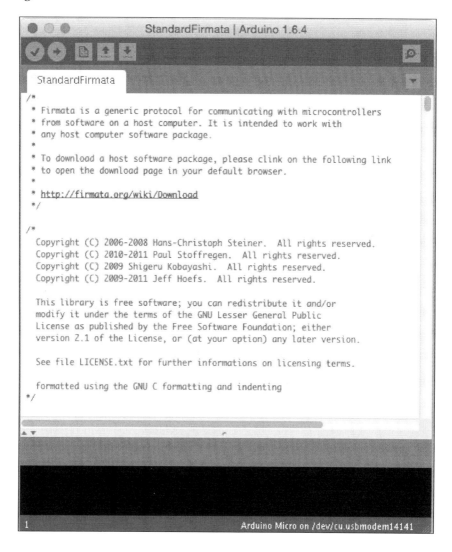

Once this sketch is up, click on the **Upload** button (it looks like an arrow pointing to the right) to upload Firmata to your board. Once the uploading is done, you can close the Arduino IDE, and you will be ready to start working with JavaScript.

A developer named Suz Hinton (@noopkat) is working on a node program called **AVRGirl** that will remove this step in the near future. Take a look at www.github.com/noopkat/avrgirl to learn more!

Hello, World! – Blinking an onboard LED

Now that we have our development environment set up, we can begin writing the JavaScript to use with our Arduino board. We'll start by blinking an LED that is already built into the Arduino microcontroller.

Writing the Johnny-Five script

In your favorite IDE, create a new `hello-world.js` file in your project directory. Then, copy and paste, or write, the following code:

```
var five = require("johnny-five");
var board = new five.Board();

board.on("ready", function() {
  var led = new five.Led(13);
  led.blink(500);
});
```

We'll go over more of what this script does in *Chapter 2*, *Working with Johnny-Five*, but the basic overview is this: we require this script in the Johnny-Five module and use it to create a new board object. When this board is ready, we will create an LED object at pin 13 (this pin is wired to the onboard LED on an Arduino Uno board). We then program this LED to blink every half second.

Running the script

In order to run the script, go to your terminal, and in your project folder, run the following:

```
node hello-world.js
```

You should see an output that looks like the following:

You should see an LED blink on your Arduino Uno. The following figure shows where the LED is on the board:

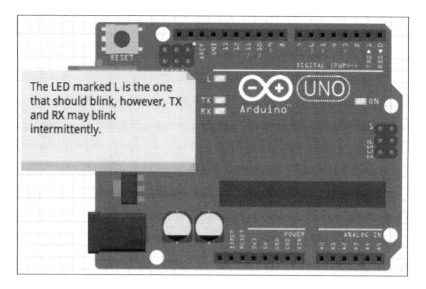

If all is well and the LED is blinking, congratulations! You're ready to start building robots and applications with Arduino and Johnny-Five!

 If there is a problem, many troubleshooting issues can be solved by checking the Johnny-Five website (www.johnny-five.io).

Summary

In this chapter, we learned about JS robotics and understood what a NodeBot is. We went through the hardware components that we will be using in the book, and we also learned how to set up the development environment. Finally, we got to know how to get the on-board LED to blink. In the next chapter, we'll dive deep into what makes Johnny-Five so powerful, and we will start writing and building some more complex projects.

2

Working with Johnny-Five

In this chapter, we'll begin working with Johnny-Five to build our own robotics projects. We'll cover what makes Johnny-Five a great library for starting with robotics, and we will build our first robot. We'll learn how we can manipulate this robot in real time from the command line—a feat not easily replicated on other platforms! By the end of this chapter, you'll have an open understanding of the software involved, which will serve as a great foundation for more complicated hardware builds.

This chapter will cover the following topics:

- How a Johnny-Five program works
- Understanding events in Johnny-Five
- Wiring an LED and making it blink
- Using **Read-Eval-Print-Loop** (**REPL**)

What you'll need for this chapter

All you'll need for this chapter is your microcontroller (the examples here still use an Arduino Uno) and a small handful of LEDs—we'll be wiring only one LED, but you may want a couple of spares, in case one burns out.

How a Johnny-Five program works

In this section, we'll take a look at the internals of a Johnny-Five program in more detail, so we can start building more complex applications.

Objects, functions, and events

Johnny-Five programs work using an event-based structure, and there are three concepts to keep in mind: objects, functions, and events.

Objects tend to programmatically represent our physical electronic components and are usually constructed using the `new` keyword. A few examples of objects in Johnny-Five include the `five` object, which represents the Johnny-Five library, the `Board` object, which represents our microcontroller; and the LED object, which will programmatically represent our LED:

```
var led = new five.Led(11);
```

Functions are available for the objects we create and usually represent the actions that our robots can do. For instance, the LED object has an `on()` and `off()` function that turns the LED on and off:

```
led.on();
led.off();
led.blink();
led.stop();
```

Events are fired on objects and represent observable points in our program. For example, the `Board` object fires a `ready` event when the board is ready to receive instructions from a Johnny-Five program.

We can also set events on a pin to track events on our LED:

```
var myPin = new five.Pin(11);
myPin.on('high', function(){
  console.log('pin 11 set to high!');
});
```

We will use all three of these concepts in every Johnny-Five program we write, so it's good to normalize our vocabulary early!

Going over our blink-LED script

In the previous chapter, we wrote a small script to blink an on-board LED on and off. Let's take a look at this code in detail and outline the objects, functions, and events we have used:

```
var five = require("johnny-five");
```

The preceding line just pulls `johnny-five` into our program so that we can use it.

```
var board = new five.Board();
```

The preceding line constructs our `board` object. Note that, without parameters, Johnny-Five assumes you are using an Arduino and guesses the serial port for you.

```
board.on("ready", function() {
  var led = new five.Led(13);
  led.blink(500);
});
```

Here, we set up a listener on our `Board` object for the `ready` event. When the board is ready, our handler instantiates an `Led` object at pin 13 and makes the LED blink by calling the `blink` function on that object.

This will be the basic format for most Johnny-Five functions: create a `Board` object, create a listener and handler for the `ready` event, and then, within the `ready` event handler, create component objects and call functions through them. We can also add listeners and handlers to the component objects—we'll talk about this in the next few chapters.

Understanding events in Johnny-Five

The events in Johnny-Five are a very important concept—this is also a new concept, especially if you are used to low-level language programming. It's very similar to the idea of interrupts, but definitely strays away from the traditional robotics programming paradigm of an event loop. While you can create timers and loops in Johnny-Five, it highly encourages an event-based programming approach, which can need some practice.

Why events?

A question that gets asked a lot is, "Why event-based? Why not loop-based and interrupt-based as in previous methods?".

A lot of this has to do with the way robots work and the way we think about how we program robots. When you think about what you want a robot to do, you're less likely to think *"Every X seconds, I want to check for A and start task B..."* and you are more likely to think *"When Y happens, I want to start event C..."*.

The event-based system in Johnny-Five works really well with this train of thought by allowing users to place listeners and handlers in the events instead of polling for the correct conditions every X seconds. It makes robotics programming a little easier to grasp for those who are new to robotics programming.

Grasping events is very important to understanding Johnny-Five—this is because every Johnny-Five script begins by instantiating a Board object and waiting for it to fire a ready event. This is the equivalent of the DOM ready event in browser-based JavaScript applications—it tells you that you're ready to start sending instructions.

Wiring up an external LED

For our first hardware project, we're going to wire an LED to the Arduino. An LED, or a Light Emitting Diode, is a component that lights up when electric current is passed through it. They come in many colors and sizes and are one of the most easy-to-use and versatile components in hobbyist robotics.

Setting up the hardware

First, take an LED. We'll determine the positive and negative leads of the LED—for this component, it's straightforward: the positive lead is longer than the negative lead.

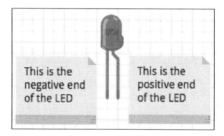

Determining the positive and negative ends of an LED

To wire the LED to an Arduino, place the positive lead on pin 11 and the negative lead on the pin marked GND, just like in the following diagram:

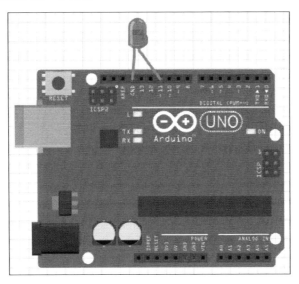

Wiring up our LED

You can also use a breadboard if you wish to—it will look like the following:

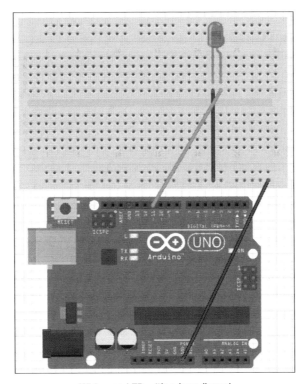

Wiring an LED with a breadboard

Now that we've wired up the LED, we're going to make it blink as we did in the last chapter. The script looks very familiar:

```
var five = require("johnny-five");

var board = new five.Board();

board.on("ready", function() {
  var led = new five.Led(11);
  led.blink(500);
});
```

This is because it's nearly the same script as in the previous chapter—we just changed the pin number to reflect the new LED we have installed.

Save and run the script. You should see a blinking LED on your board, as shown in the following screenshot:

[TODO: Add Photo]

When you run the script, you'll notice a prompt—you can even type into it! This is the REPL, and we're going to use it to play with our LED in real time!

Using the Read-Eval-Print-Loop (REPL)

The Read, Eval, Print Loop, or REPL, is a concept relative to many scripting languages, but it is new to libraries, and definitely new to robotics. Think about how you alter the state in a typical Arduino program: you modify the source code, re-load it onto the board, and wait for it to run.

However, due to the way Johnny-Five works, we can modify the state of our robot code *while the code is running.* This is because we use Firmata—the board is just a thin client that reacts to instructions from our node program, so if we let our Node programs send different instructions, we can change how our robot works in real time.

The way to do this in a Johnny-Five program is by injecting components into the REPL, which allows us to use them.

Making components available to the REPL

We're going to modify our script from the previous section in order to manipulate our LED. To do this, we're going to use the `this.repl.inject()` function. The `this` keyword, when used within our `board.on('ready')` handler, is a reference to the global context, so we can access the REPL for the program we are working on with `this.repl`. The `inject` method accepts an object; the keys of this object will represent the names you can access from the REPL, and the values will be the components you wish to access.

So, we're going to pass the following object to the `inject` method. It will allow us to access our LED component by the `myLed` name:

```
{
  myLed: led
}
```

Our new program looks like this:

```
var five = require("johnny-five");

var board = new five.Board();

board.on("ready", function() {
  var led = new five.Led(11);

  this.repl.inject({
    myLed: led
  });

  led.blink(500);
});
```

Go ahead and save this in `LED-repl.js`. Now we have the code that we had before — the LED at pin 11 will blink — but we have programmatic access to this LED via the REPL. Now, let's run it and have some fun.

Using the REPL

First, with the LED still wired to pin 11, attach your board to your computer. Then, in your command line, in the same folder as your `.js` file, run the following:

```
> node LED-repl.js
```

You should see a boot-up sequence, followed by a prompt—it'll look like the following screenshot. Your LED wired to pin 11 should also start blinking.

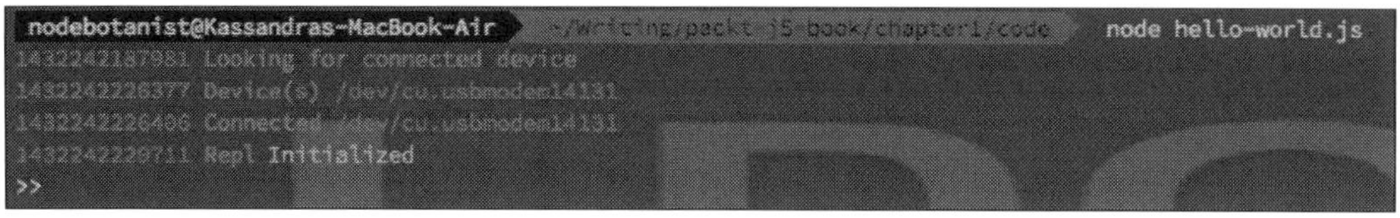

The terminal setup for the Johnny-Five REPL prompt

This (as well as the **Repl Initialized** line) means that you can start working with the REPL. Try typing myLed and hit *Enter*. What you'll see is an object representing your LED:

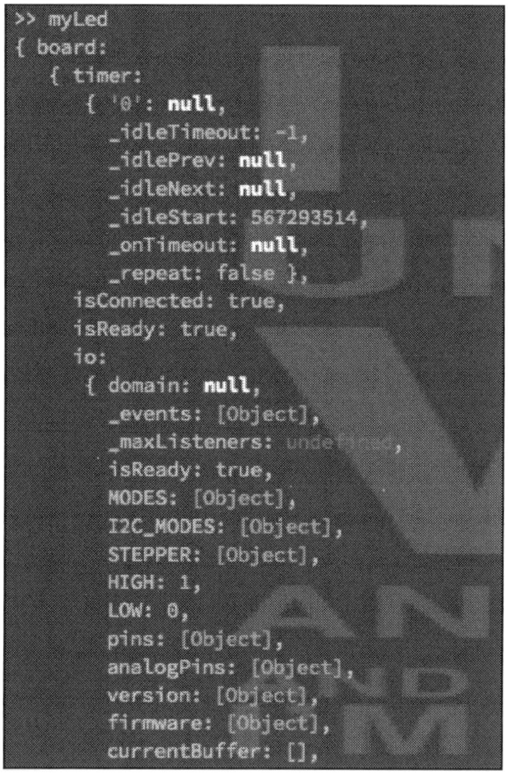

The output of your myLed object in the REPL

You can see the names of several functions and attributes of the LED object. Next, we'll use the REPL to stop the blinking of the LED. Type myLed.stop() into the REPL and hit *Enter*. As the .stop() function returns the LED object, the output will look like the following screenshot:

```
>> myLed.stop()
{ board:
   { timer:
      { '0': null,
        _idleTimeout: -1,
        _idlePrev: null,
        _idleNext: null,
        _idleStart: 567293514,
        _onTimeout: null,
        _repeat: false },
     isConnected: true,
     isReady: true,
     io:
      { domain: null,
        _events: [Object],
        _maxListeners: undefined,
        isReady: true,
        MODES: [Object],
        I2C_MODES: [Object],
        STEPPER: [Object],
```

The output from `myLed.stop();`

This function should return quickly, and the LED will stop blinking.

Please note that the LED will not necessarily turn off;
it may just stay on.

One of the cool things about Johnny-Five's object functions is that they are chainable—
if you want the LED to remain off once you stop its blinking, you can use `myLed.`
`stop().off()`:

```
>> myLed.stop().off()
{ board:
   { timer:
      { '0': null,
        _idleTimeout: -1,
        _idlePrev: null,
        _idleNext: null,
        _idleStart: 567293514,
        _onTimeout: null,
        _repeat: false },
     isConnected: true,
     isReady: true,
     io:
      { domain: null,
        _events: [Object],
        _maxListeners: undefined,
        isReady: true,
        MODES: [Object],
        I2C_MODES: [Object],
        STEPPER: [Object],
```

Using chainable function calls in the REPL

There are a bunch of LED functions available to you in the REPL:

- `.on()` and `.off()`
- `.blink()`
- `.pulse()`
- `.toggle()`
- `.strobe()`
- `.fadeIn()` and `.fadeOut()`

Try them all to see what happens with your `myLed` object!

Summary

In this chapter, we learned how to wire up an LED and how to use the REPL to modify our robot's state in real time. We understood what software is involved when working with complex hardware. We also looked at what makes Johnny-Five stand out in the robotics world by exploring the REPL and the event structure of Johnny-Five programs.

In the next chapter, we'll explore pins — including analog and PWM pins — and talk more about how an LED can be set to different values of brightness.

3
Using Digital and PWM Output Pins

In this chapter, we'll explore the pins of our microcontroller: how they work, how to manipulate them with Johnny-Five, and how different pins can be programmed to behave in different ways. We'll also build two new projects—one in which we will use several LEDs to explore the Led API more, and another in which we will use a Piezo element to make some music! We will cover the following topics in this chapter:

- How GPIO pins work
- Using multiple outputs with several LEDs
- Using a PWM output with a Piezo element

What you'll need for this chapter

For the first project, you'll need your microcontroller, a handful of breadboard wires, a half-sized breadboard, and five LEDs.

For the second project, you'll need your microcontroller, a handful of breadboard wires, a half-sized breadboard, and a Piezo element.

How GPIO pins work

If we look at our last project, we can observe from the code that we're writing values to an Led object in Johnny-Five, and it's changing the state and brightness of an LED. How does this work? While the in-depth details are beyond the scope of this book, we will go a little into how this works; this uses the concept of **GPIO**, or **General-Purpose Input/Output**, pins.

A GPIO pin is a pin that provides electric current to or reads electric current from a circuit. In our last project, we used this to provide varying levels of power to our LED. These pins can be configured by users (that's us!) to be used as input (read electric current) or output (provide electric current). For now, we're going to focus on the output pins, of which there are two main types: Digital and PWM.

Digital output pins

Digital output pins are only capable of providing two levels of electric current to our circuits: 1 and 0, HI and LOW, or ON and OFF. This means if we plug an LED into a digital pin, we can only turn it on or off.

However, in our case, when we ran the pulse() method, our LED exhibited varying levels of brightness. What does this mean? This means we used a PWM pin in our previous examples.

PWM output pins

A **PWM (Pulse-Width Modulation)** pin is capable of sending varying levels of power to our circuit (sort of). The way this works is actually by setting the pin to HIGH and then LOW very quickly in a timed manner, which emulates varying levels of power.

Programmatically, you can set a PWM pin to any value between 0 and 255, inclusive. The value you set the pin to decides how often the pin is set to HIGH; for instance, the value 0 would mean the PWM pin is set to HIGH for 0% of the time. The value 85 is one-third of 255, and would mean the pin is set to HIGH for one-third of the time—this emulates one-third power, or in the case of our LED, one-third brightness.

Our first example uses a PWM pin to show varying degrees of brightness of our LED, but there are nearly infinite uses for PWM pins—as we'll see later in this chapter, we can even make music with them!

How to tell the difference between Digital and PWM pins

How can you check which pins are PWM on a microcontroller? This really depends on the microcontroller you're using. For the Arduino Uno, which we have used in this book, the PWM pins are marked with a ~, or tilde, symbol. This means, on an Uno, the PWM pins are 3, 5, 6, 9, 10, and 11.

Determining the PWM pins on an Arduino Uno

Next, we'll explore the differences between the pins by wiring up several LEDs and playing with the Led API.

Multiple pins with several LEDs

For the next project, we're going to look at the Led object API and test several different methods. This is one of the benefits of Johnny-Five—abstraction. If you can understand the concept of an LED, you can use the Johnny-Five LED object without thinking about the underlying pins or timings. Let's go over the methods that we'll use for our project:

- on() and off(): These turn an LED on and off. Under abstraction, this sets the pin that is wired to the LED to HIGH and LOW, respectively. We'll be using these in the REPL.

- blink(time): This turns an LED on and off at a given interval. strobe() and blink() are aliases of each other and do the same thing.

- pulse(time): This will cause an LED to pulse on and off in an eased manner. This requires an LED wired to a PWM pin. The time argument sets the length of each side of the pulse—500 will mean the LED will fade in for 500 ms and fade out for 500 ms, meaning a 1-second pulse.

- fade(brightness, ms): This will cause an LED to fade on or off from its current brightness to the given brightness over ms milliseconds.

- stop(): This stops any recurring action happening on an LED. Note that this won't necessarily turn off the LED. It will stop the action in its tracks—if this means the LED is on, so be it.

Remember that most Johnny-Five object functions are chainable—you can use one right after the other.

```
myLed1.stop().off()
```

The preceding code will stop any recurring event on the LED and then turn it off.

Now that we know what functions we'll be working with, let's wire up our next project.

Setting up the hardware for the project

Grab your materials and look at the following diagram:

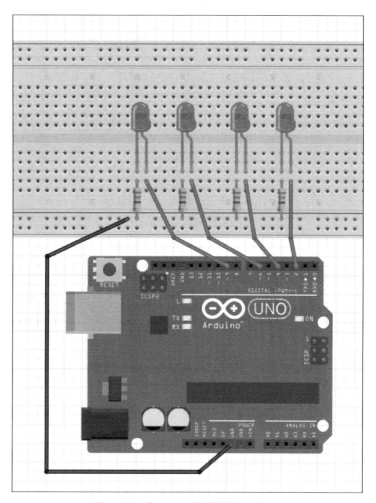

The wiring for our multiple LEDs project

Note that the LEDs are wired to pins 2, 4, 6, and 9—two on Digital pins and two on PWM pins. We will perform an experiment to check whether they are Digital or PWM pins.

Writing the script for the project

Let's write our script, called `leds-gpio.js`, with the following objectives in mind:

1. Establish the `Board` object and add a handler to the board's `ready` event.
2. Create `Led` objects for each of our LEDs.
3. Make the LEDs on pins 2 and 9 accessible to the REPL as `myLed2` and `myLed9` respectively.
4. Set the LED on pin 4 to blink every 500 ms.
5. Set the LED on pin 6 to pulse every 500 ms.

Your code should look like this:

```
var five = require("johnny-five");

var board = new five.Board();

board.on("ready", function() {
  var myLed2 = new five.Led(2);
  var myLed4 = new five.Led(4);
  var myLed6 = new five.Led(6);
  var myLed9 = new five.Led(9);

  this.repl.inject({
    myLed2: myLed2,
    myLed9: myLed9
  });

  myLed4.blink(500);
  myLed6.pulse(500);
});
```

Now, let's run the script and play around with our new `Led` objects.

Exploring more about LED objects in Johnny-Five

When you run the script, the LEDs on pins 4 and 6 should start blinking and pulsing, respectively. First, let's see what happens when we run `pulse()`, a method that requires a PWM pin, on our LED wired to pin 2, which is a digital pin. In the REPL, run the following:

```
myLed2.pulse(500);
```

You should be promptly kicked out of the REPL as your program crashes.

An error when using a PWM method on a digital pin

This is because Johnny-Five watches your program and makes sure that you don't try to use PWM methods on digital pins. This also shows one of the other benefits of Johnny-Five—the maintainers have taken great pains to make sure that many error messages are clear, which can be an issue while dealing with robotics code.

Restart your code, and run the following:

```
myLed2.on().isOn
```

This will return the value as `true` in your REPL:

```
>> myLed2.on().isOn
true
```

The isOn attribute

This points to an attribute of the `Led` object. `isOn` tells you whether the LED is on (any value other than `0`) or off (a `0` value). There are other attributes of your LED:

```
>> myLed2.value
1
>> myLed2.isOn
true
>>
```

The other LED attributes

Go ahead and explore these attributes and the function with `myLed2` and `myLed9`.

Now that we've learned how to use one of the less complicated Johnny-Five components, the LED, let's take a look at a component with a more interesting API and make some music with the Piezo object.

Using PWM pins with the Piezo element

Piezo elements can be really fun—you can use them to simply add music to your Johnny-Five projects. We're going to build a small project and play with some of the Johnny-Five utilities to make music with this fun little component.

Setting up the hardware

Wiring a Piezo is pretty straightforward—you need to determine the + and - sides first. Usually, the + side is marked on the top of the plastic casing of the Piezo, and one leg is longer—much like an LED, the longer leg denotes the + side. Finally, some Piezo buzzers come with lead wires that are red (the + side) and black (the - side).

Once you've determined the + side, wire it to pin 3, and wire the - side to **GND**, as shown in the following diagram:

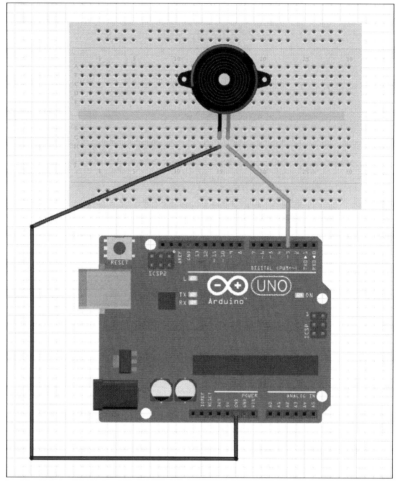

A Piezo wiring diagram

Writing the script

The script is a little more complicated than our last few scripts; we need to create a Piezo element, which just requires a pin. However, a piece of music is more complicated than turning an LED on and off. Luckily, the Johnny-Five Piezo API has the play() method, which takes an object. This object has attributes such as beats, tempo, and song—we'll use these to play our tune.

There are many ways to describe a song for the play() method. One way—the way that we'll use here—is as a string of notes, as follows:

C D F D A - A A A A G G G G - - C D F D G - G G G G F F F F - -

When you use this method, it will assume the middle octave, and the - symbol indicates null or off notes—nothing will play here.

For beats, we will use one-fourth time, and for tempo, we'll start with 100 bpm (beats per minute). Your code will look like this:

```
var five = require("johnny-five"),
  board = new five.Board();

board.on("ready", function() {
  var piezo = new five.Piezo(3);

  board.repl.inject({
    piezo: piezo
  });

  piezo.play({
    song: "C D F D A - A A A A G G G G - - C D F D G -
      G G G G F F F F - -",
    beats: 1 / 4,
    tempo: 20
  });

});
```

Save it to a file called piezo.js and run it in your terminal:

node piezo.js

You should hear a jaunty tune come from your Arduino board!

What's going on with the pin?

The reason a Piezo requires a PWM pin is that the Piezo object is sending different amounts of power through pin 3 to the Piezo, which causes it to emit different notes. The Johnny-Five library allows us to show these notes in a way that we can understand, instead of having to calculate how much power to send for each note.

Exploring the Piezo API

You can now explore the Piezo API further, including looking at the other ways of writing tunes that give you more control of the octave. Check the Johnny-Five website for more details and examples.

A challenge: using the REPL, find a way to make the Piezo stop playing mid song. A hint: there is a `piezo.off()` method.

Summary

In this chapter, we explored how GPIO pins work and how they form the underpinnings of Johnny-Five objects by manipulating pin values.

Next, we'll look at how to handle input in the Johnny-Five projects with analog input pins.

4

Using Specialized
Output Devices

Now that we know how output pins (both digital and PWM) work, we're going to take a look at specialized output devices. These devices use multiple pins for one device for a number of reasons: some use protocols that are widely known, some are proprietary, some just require a lot of pins to output a lot of data. We'll take a look at a few of the well-known protocols and build a project with one such device: a character LCD, reminiscent of a calculator. This chapter will cover the following topics:

- Outputs that require multiple pins
- Checking compatibility with Johnny-Five
- Obtaining documentation, wiring diagrams, and so on
- Project – character LCD display

What you'll need for this chapter

For the project in this chapter, you'll need your board, a USB cable, and a character LCD character display. A breadboard and a handful of breadboard wires will also come in handy.

We will go over how to use character LCDs with or without an I2C interface. An example of one with an I2C interface can be found here: `http://www.amazon.com/SainSmart-Serial-Module-Display-Arduino/dp/B00813HBEQ`. A way to quickly identify an I2C-compatible character LCD is by the backpack that is presoldered on to it, as shown in the following examples. It only uses four pins labeled as **VCC**, **GND**, **SDA**, and **SCL**:

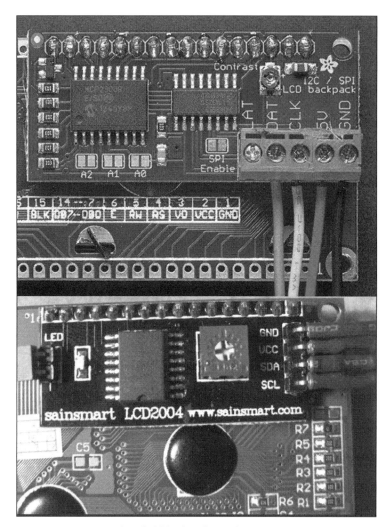

Examples of I2C backpacks on character LCDs

An example of a character LCD without an I2C interface is available here: `https://www.adafruit.com/products/181`. The main visible difference is that these character LCDs use more than the four pins used by I2C interfaces.

Note that these may also require assembly by soldering!

The following screenshot is an example of this:

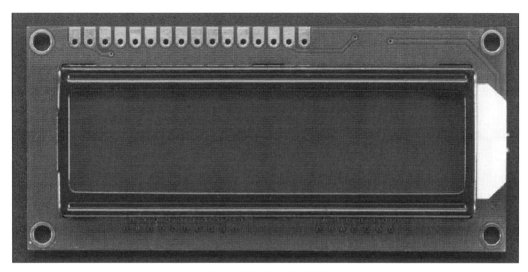

A non-I2C character LCD

Note that if you are using a board that is *NOT* an Arduino, read the section on checking compatibility *BEFORE* buying your character LCD—you'll want to make sure that your board is I2C-compatible beforehand. All Arduino boards used here had I2C compatibility with Johnny-Five at the time of writing this book.

Outputs that require multiple pins

There are many types of output, many of which only need one output pin for data, such as LEDs and the Piezo element that we used in the last few chapters. However, there are nearly an infinite number of output devices that we can use—many of them require more complicated instructions than one output pin is capable of sending.

These devices work in several different ways, and while the exact ways are well beyond the scope of this book, we'll go over a few very common types. For this chapter, however, we'll just go over the I2C, because it is the common format for the device that we will use in this chapter's project.

Inter-Integrated Circuits (I2C)

I2C, or Inter-Integrated Circuits, are output devices that can share the same set of two data pins. The data pins are usually called **SCL (Serial Clock Line)** and **SDA (Serial Data Line)**, where SCL handles timing and SDA sends data. The reason you can wire many devices to one pair of digital output pins is because in order to send or receive a message from an I2C device, you need to know its address—a hexadecimal byte prefaced to every message to the device that determines which device the message is meant for.

I2C is also commonly used for input devices that have a lot of data to send, such as some accelerometers and magnetometers, as we'll see in the next chapter.

Checking compatibility with Johnny-Five

It's easy to find a lot of different devices online, but how do you know what will work with Johnny-Five? and will it work on Johnny-Five for your particular board?

Luckily, the Johnny-Five website at www.johnny-five.io can easily tell you this, and you just need to follow a few steps in order to determine what type of device you are looking at.

First, let's take a look at the website at www.johnny-five.io. There are several tabs, but for now, we're looking for the **Platform Support** tab:

The johnny-five.io header

Once you are on the **Platform Support** page, look for the board you're using. If you're using Arduino Uno, your search should be short—it's at the top of the page!

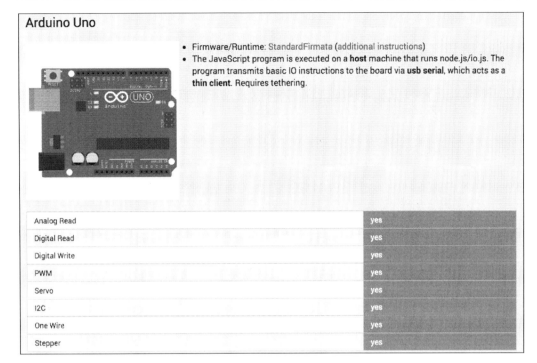

Arduino Uno

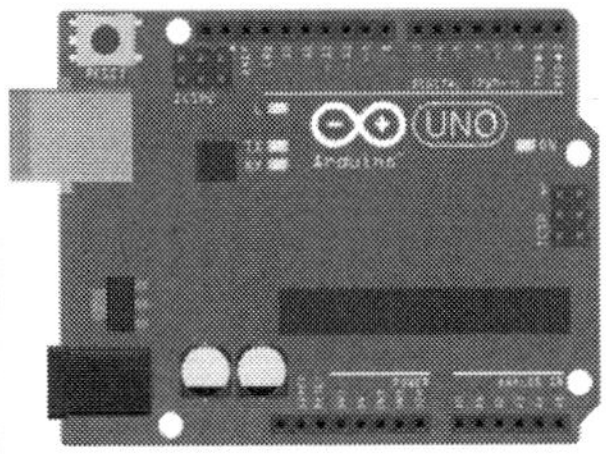

- Firmware/Runtime: StandardFirmata (additional instructions)
- The JavaScript program is executed on a **host** machine that runs node.js/io.js. The program transmits basic IO instructions to the board via **usb serial**, which acts as a **thin client**. Requires tethering.

Analog Read	yes
Digital Read	yes
Digital Write	yes
PWM	yes
Servo	yes
I2C	yes
One Wire	yes
Stepper	yes

The Platform Support page entry for Arduino Uno

As you can see, there's a table for compatibility with each board entry. If you're not using an Arduino Uno, quickly check whether or not your board has I2C compatibility before buying or trying to use an I2C character LCD.

Obtaining documentation, wiring diagrams, and so on

A good skill to have when building your own Johnny-Five projects is finding code and wiring diagrams for the components that you'd like to use. Luckily, the `www.johnny-five.io` website and the project provide a thorough and top-notch documentation right there on the site!

Let's take a look at the LCD documentation on the site to prepare us for building our project:

1. In the header of the site, click on the **API** tab.
2. Then, you'll see a list of components on the left (if you're on a desktop) or at the top (if you're on a tablet or phone).

3. Find and click the LCD entry in this list.

API Documentation

Component Classes

Accelerometer

Animation

Barometer

Board

Guides

- **Getting Started** Get Johnny-Five alive on your machine. (es_ES, nl_NL, pt_BR, fr_FR)
- **Prerequisites** Prerequisites for Linux, OSX, and Windows.
- **IO Plugins** Create IO Plugins for any platform!
- **Control System Hierarchy Overview** A terminology primer for component class and IO Plugin authors.

The API documentation page

Once you are on the LCD page, you'll see a bunch of different LCD components, a section on the LCD API, and some links to examples at the bottom. There is a page like this for every component in Johnny-Five, so it's easy to find out how to get started with just about every component that has already been adapted.

Let's take a look at the LCD API that we'll use to work on our next project.

The constructor takes several parameters, depending on the type of LCD you are using. We'll cover the pin options in detail when we build our project, but rows and columns are something that we can knock out now. Whether you can read it from the packaging or estimate it by looking at the number of character spaces, go ahead and figure out how many rows and columns you have on your LCD.

There's also a backlight pin option; most LCDs have a backlight and some have an RGB backlight. If you have no backlight, you do not need to initialize this parameter; if you have a single-color backlight, you'll want to note that you need to set this option.

If you have an LCD with an RGB backlight, you'll want to look at the `Led.RGB` class under the LED subheader and instantiate this yourself—we'll take a peek at the actual code for this in the project section, but go ahead and look at the RGB LED API to just be sure.

Once you've made yourself familiar with looking up information on the Johnny-Five website, you'll have unlocked a wide range of information for your projects. Is something missing? The entire page is open source and available on GitHub (`https://github.com/bocoup/johnny-five.io`), so you can file issues and make pull requests with your own examples.

Project – character LCD display

For our project, we're going to connect our character LCD to our Arduino Uno board and use Johnny-Five to print some messages on it. I'll be using an I2C display, but will include wiring diagrams and code for non-I2C versions as well.

Wiring up – I2C LCDs

First, we'll describe how to wire up an I2C LCD. Note that the image diagram will look different, because no component exists in the imaging software for the I2C backpack. There is an accompanying diagram to clarify your queries.

You'll want to look for the pins labeled SCL and SDA on the back of your LCD unit—these pins need to be connected to two pins on the Arduino Uno that are not clearly labeled on all units. These pins are near the USB connector and the reset button. With the USB connector facing left, the pins are on the left-most side of the top rail of pins—on the left is SCL, and on the right is SDA. On newer boards, these are labeled on the side of the pin railing.

Once these are in place, you'll want to connect VCC to 5 V and GND to GND. If an LED pin exists, you can wire it to 3v3.

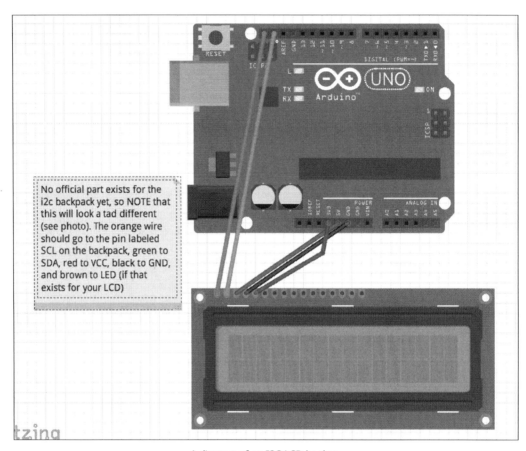

No official part exists for the i2c backpack yet, so NOTE that this will look a tad different (see photo). The orange wire should go to the pin labeled SCL on the backpack, green to SDA, red to VCC, black to GND, and brown to LED (if that exists for your LCD)

A diagram of an I2C LCD hookup

The photo of an I2C backpack wiring – wiring up regular LCDs

There are six data pins and a few ground and power pins to use when wiring a non-I2C LCD. These pins are **rs**, **en**, **d4**, **d5**, **d6**, and **d7**, and are represented by pins **4**, **6**, **11**, **12**, **13**, and **14** on the LCD. We're going to wire these to pins **8**, **9**, **4**, **5**, **6**, and **7** on the Uno.

Pins **2** and **15** are both connected to the main power supply—pin **2** powers the LCD itself, and pin **15** powers the backlight LED. Pins **1** and **16** run to ground to match pins **2** and **15**. Pin **3** is connected to a potentiometer—about which we'll talk more in the next chapter. For now, note that it looks like a small turnable knob. You should have received one with your LCD, and you should, for now, wire it up as shown in the following diagram—the left-hand side to power, the right-hand side to ground, and the middle to pin **3** of the LCD (note—you can't get this backwards). This potentiometer controls contrast, and is built into I2C LCDs.

Please note that, in the following diagram, the Arduino Uno has been rotated. Please be sure to be careful while wiring this up!

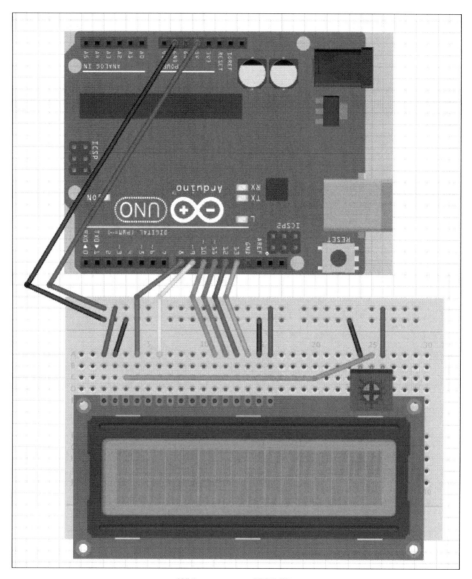

Wiring up a non-I2C LCD

In order to check that your wiring is working, you can plug your Arduino into your computer. The backlight should turn on, and you should be able to see block characters on your LCD. Adjust the potentiometer, if necessary, to see the block characters.

The code

Now that we have our LCD wired up, we're going to write some code in the following sections. While we will do some initialization in the code, we will also open up the LCD to the REPL and play with it in real time!

The I2C version

The code for the I2C version LCD is as follows:

```
var five = require("johnny-five");
var board = new five.Board();

board.on("ready", function() {
  // Controller: PCF8574A (Generic I2C)
  // Locate the controller chip model number on the chip itself.
  var l = new five.LCD({
    controller: "PCF8574A",
  });

  this.repl.inject({
    lcd: l
  })

  l.useChar("heart");
  l.cursor(0, 0).print("hello :heart:");
  l.blink();
});
```

The non-I2C version

The code for the non-I2C version LCD is as follows:

```
var five = require("johnny-five");
var board = new five.Board();

board.on("ready", function() {
  var l = new five.LCD({
    pins: [8, 9, 10, 11, 12, 13]
  });

  this.repl.inject({
    lcd: l
  })
```

```
    l.useChar("heart");
    l.cursor(0, 0).print("hello :heart:");
    l.blink();
  });
```

Remember, use the I2C version if your LCD has an I2C backpack; otherwise, use the non-I2C version. The difference between them is the controller; the I2C LCD requires a controller that will be listed on the backpack, whereas non-I2C requires an array of pins used to control the LCD.

Running the code

Now that we've written the code, let's start the program. Use the `lcd-i2c.js` node or the `lcd.js` node, depending on the type of character LCD you are using to start the program.

What you should see is your LCD lighting up and displaying **hello**, followed by a heart character. The LCD carat should be also blinking.

Where did the heart character come from? One of the many fun things about character LCDs is that you can define quite a few custom icons to use with them. Johnny-Five has created a set that you can use in the `lcd` object. Some other examples of icons defined by Johnny-Five include target, duck, dice1, dice2, up to dice6, and check.

 Please note that you can only use up to eight of these custom characters at one time—LCDs have a limited memory for custom characters.

Now that our code is running, we're going to play around with the LCD API using the REPL. We've attached our `lcd` object to the `lcd` variable. First, let's clear the LCD as follows:

```
> lcd.clear();
```

Your LCD should now be blank, and the carat should still be blinking. If you'd like to turn this off, you can type the following:

```
> lcd.noBlink();
```

This will turn off the carat. Want to start on line 2? We can move the cursor with the `cursor(row, column)` function:

```
>lcd.cursor(1, 0);
```

Similar to arrays and other programming concepts, the column and row indices of an LCD are 0-based: for example, row 2 is index 1. Now, let's print something on row 2:

```
>lcd.print("hello, world!");
```

This should print properly on the second line. Now, let's clear the display, so we can show an edge case of character LCDs:

```
> lcd.clear();
>lcd.print("This is a really really really really long sentence!");
```

Notice anything weird? When line 1 overflows, it starts printing on row 3, and then row 2. This is how the LCD functions normally. What this means is that you'll need to check the length of what you print to prevent this overflow from making your code look broken. Now, let's clear our LCD and load one of the custom characters for our own use:

```
>lcd.clear();
>lcd.useChar('clock');
>lcd.print(":clock:");
```

This will clear the LCD and print a clock character. The `.useChar` function pulls the character with this name out of the definitions that Johnny-Five provides and sends the commands to the LCD to load it into memory. When we run the `.print` function, the `":"` delimiters tell the function that we want to use a special character.

Summary

In this chapter, we've looked at how to use specialized inputs by walking through the documentation on `johnny-five.io`. The knowledge used here will allow you to use many different components that you come across in your robotics adventures. Just be sure that, if you find a new component and write the code, you contribute it back to Johnny-Five to make it better for everyone else!

In the next chapter, we will learn how to use many different input devices and sensors in order to build Johnny-Five projects.

5
Using Input Devices and Sensors

We've handled outputs, but what makes robots truly interesting is the use of inputs to generate outputs! In this chapter, we'll go over basic input devices, such as buttons, and environmental sensors, such as a sensor that detects ambient light. We'll talk about how Johnny-Five uses events to make these devices easy to use, and build some projects. After finishing this chapter, you should have all the knowledge that you need to handle most input/output projects.

This chapter will cover the following topics:

- How analog input pins work
- Johnny-Five's sensor events
- Using basic inputs – buttons and potentiometers
- Using sensors – light and temperature
- Other types of sensors and their uses

What you'll need for this chapter

For the project in this chapter, you'll need your board, a USB cable, and a few inputs and sensors.

First, you'll want a button. You can find these aplenty in most starter kits, but you can also buy them separately. We're going to consider a button with a four-prong design, as shown in the following screenshot:

A common push button for robotics projects

However, a design with two prongs is fine too—four-prong buttons still represent two sides of the button, so you can replicate these with two-prong designs.

You'll also need a rotating potentiometer—these are knobs that you twist to set a value, similar to the volume knob on a speaker. You'll want one that's breadboard-friendly with a three-prong design, as shown in the following screenshot:

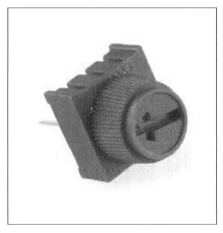

A basic rotating potentiometer

Please note that you may have access to a sliding potentiometer (one that looks like a sliding switch or similar to a dimmer switch) or some other potentiometer. These will work fine, but check the www.johnny-five.io site for more details on wiring them.

For inputs, first you'll need a light sensor that is commonly referred to as a photocell. Usually, these look like diodes that are tan with a wave design on top, as shown in the following screenshot:

A light sensor diode

There are breakout boards for light sensors as well, but for this chapter, let's stick with the diode kind. These can be found very easily on Adafruit and SparkFun.

To round out our sensors, you'll want a temperature sensor. These look like small, half-cut cylinders with three metal prongs at the bottom. I recommend the TMP36, which has TMP written on the back, as shown in the following screenshot:

A temperature sensor

You can also use a LM35 with the same wiring—this sensor looks the same as the TMP36, except that LM35 is written on the back. If you use a different temperature sensor, before you continue, be sure to check the johnny-five.io documentation at http://johnny-five.io/api/temperature to see whether or not the sensor is supported.

You'll also need a breadboard, a handful of breadboard wires, an LED, and a few 10k Ohm resistors.

Resistors lower the electric current being sent to our sensors to ensure accurate readings and are also sometimes used to protect output devices. To make sure that your resistors are 10k ohm, we're going to use the colored stripes on the resistor. Your resistor should have brown, black, and orange bands. There may be another band after these—the color of this band, for our purposes, doesn't matter. The resistor should look like the following:

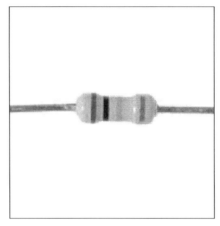

A 10k ohm resistor

How analog input pins work

Inputs are the first half of awesome robots equations; robots that know the weather, can tell how fast they are moving, or see where things are. Input pins make this possible, so in this section we'll discuss how they work and how we're going to utilize them.

Analog input pins work by reading a voltage level from a sensor and converting this voltage level to an integer value between 0 and 1,023. Input device manufacturers usually give a scale to their device that tells us how to turn this integer value into a real-world value; for instance, we'll do this with our temperature sensor to change the value into a temperature that we as humans can understand.

We're going to utilize these pins by plugging in both the human input devices and the environmental sensors, and map ping the inputs that they give. This way, we can start developing projects that use inputs to generate outputs.

Johnny-Five sensor events

As discussed in the previous chapters, Johnny-Five is dependent on events for a lot of its functionality. This is not different for inputs and sensors—most of the time, you'll interact with these by waiting for events. While most input devices have ways way to read data at any given moment, these are mostly used for debugging, and you'll need to have a good grasp of the events available for your input device or sensor when coding your projects.

Most input devices and sensors have a `data` event; this event tells the program when data is read from the device. This is a kind of a firehose: it reports quite quickly and can be a little overwhelming. This is usually used for debugging, as most robotics programs are more interested in when the sensor or input data changes rather than when there is new input to be read.

The `change` event, also available on most devices, is a very commonly-used event—it only fires when the incoming data has changed. A good example is a temperature change as we'll see in one of the projects in this chapter.

The best way to figure out what events to use is by the Johnny-Five documentation for your device at `johnny-five.io`; this will give you a full list of events for each input and sensor type and can be very helpful when starting new projects.

Using basic inputs – buttons and potentiometers

Let's take a look at using some basic input devices first. We'll start with a button and a potentiometer—two of the easiest input devices to use with Johnny-Five, and a good way to get acquainted with both specialized input objects, such as buttons, and general `Sensor` objects, which we'll use for the potentiometer.

Wiring up our button and LED

First, we're going to wire up a button and write some code to measure whether it is pressed or not, using an LED as our indicator. The wiring of the project will look like this:

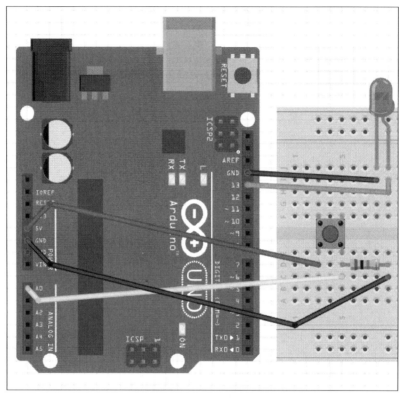

Wiring diagram for a button and an LED

Make sure that if you're using the four-prong button, it crosses over the center trough of your breadboard as shown in the diagram. If it does not, the button will not work properly. If you are using a two-prong button, the wiring is very similar, and it does not have to cross over.

Coding button-led.js

Now, let's take a look at the Button object in Johnny Five to see what we'll need to use for our code. First, we want to see whether or not there's an event to tap into when the button is pressed. Sure enough, there is such an event: the press event is logged when the button is pressed. Right below this, we see the release event that is logged when the button is released.

Using these and our previous knowledge of the `Led` object, we can write the following in `button-led.js`:

```
var five = require('johnny-five');

var board = new five.Board();

board.on('ready', function(){
  var button = new five.Button('A0');
  var led = new five.Led(13);

  button.on('press', function(){
    console.log('button pressed!');
    led.on();
  });

  button.on('release', function(){
    console.log('button released!');
    led.off();
  })
});
```

This code will light the LED when the button is pressed and turn it off again when the button is released. Go ahead and run it with the following command:

```
> node button-led.js
```

Try this out. You should see an output in your console like the following:

The output from led-button.js

The LED should be lit when the button is pressed, and it should be turned off when the button is released.

Now that we've got a button working, let's set up our potentiometer and discover some other events related to input and sensor devices. Our project will set the brightness of the LED to correlate to the input from the potentiometer—we're building a dimmer switch, essentially.

Wiring the potentiometer and the LED

Grab your potentiometer and follow the wiring in the following diagram:

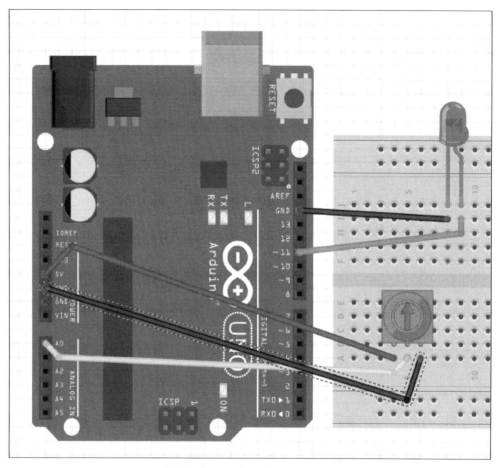

Wiring diagram for a dimmer switch

 Please note that if you're using the setup from your button project, the **LED** pin changes in this one, so make sure that you move it, too.

Coding our dimmer switch

As we write our code, you'll notice that there is no potentiometer object in Johnny-Five. That's fine. As the potentiometer is a very basic sensor, we'll be using the Sensor object instead.

Next, let's take a look at the events that we'll be using. The change event fires when the input from the potentiometer changes, so we'll use this event to trigger our LED change. In order to get the reading, we'll use this.value, as explained in the documentation.

Now, let's think about how LEDs work and about the input from the potentiometer. The LED can be set from 0 to 255, and the potentiometer can take an input from 0 to 1023. We can do the math to scale these inputs ourselves, but luckily, Johnny-Five has a function to help us out. This is called the scale(min, max) function. It will scale our input to the number that we give it; in our case, 0 and 255. We will still use this.value to reference the scaled value. If you want to see the unscaled value in the event handler, you can use this.raw.

We can use the scale function before the event listener call to scale our potentiometer's output to the range our LED can understand.

With this in mind, we can write the code for our dimmer switch. Go ahead and place the following code in dimmer-switch.js:

```
var five = require('johnny-five');

var board = new five.Board();

board.on('ready', function(){
  var pot = new five.Sensor('A0');
  var led = new five.Led(11);

  pot.scale(0, 255).on('change', function(){
    console.log('The scaled potentiometer value is: ' +
      this.value);
    console.log('The raw potentiometer value is: ' + this.raw);
    led.brightness(this.value);
  });
});
```

Start the script using the following:

```
> node dimmer-switch.js
```

Try this out by twisting the potentiometer. Data should log in to your terminal as follows:

```
The scaled potentiometer value is: 74.37396244634874
The raw potentiometer value is: 301.6830960523803
The scaled potentiometer value is: 74.62085480079986
The raw potentiometer value is: 302.8240005893167
The scaled potentiometer value is: 74.09539178735577
The raw potentiometer value is: 300.57111365231685
The scaled potentiometer value is: 74.63298110873438
The raw potentiometer value is: 301.508853206411
The scaled potentiometer value is: 74.48949674842879
The raw potentiometer value is: 301.591794724809
The scaled potentiometer value is: 74.6783123346977
The raw potentiometer value is: 302.1139590013772
```

The output from dimmer-switch.js

The brightness of the LED should change accordingly. Now that we have a good grasp on input devices, we'll take a look at sensors, using a photocell and a temperature sensor.

Using sensors – Light and Temperature

Now, we'll build a couple of projects that demonstrate how to use more advanced sensors: a **photocell** and a **temperature** sensor. We'll learn how specialized Johnny-Five `Sensor` objects allow us to make these easier to use, and how to play with inputs in the REPL and show some input data in the console using a module called `barcli`.

Wiring up our photocell

First, we'll start with the photocell—see the following wiring diagram:

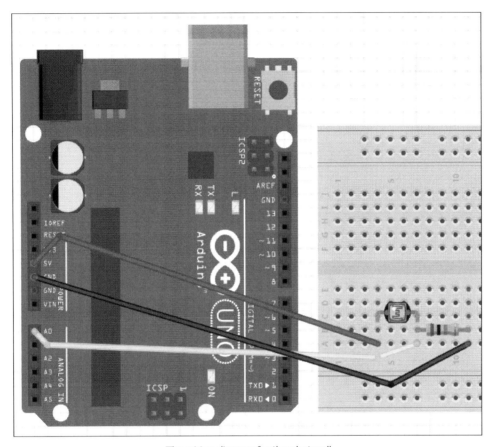

The wiring diagram for the photocell

 Note that the resistor setup is how we wire up a sensor with only two leads and we need three—input, power, and ground.

Coding our photocell example

As we code our photocell example, we'll note that there is no photocell object, so we're going to use the generic Sensor object, as we did with the potentiometer.

As for outputting the data that we get from the sensor, we're going to use a handy utility called **barcli** to make our output much easier to read.

barcli

In the early days of Johnny-Five, one of the most common ways to check sensor data was to log the data on every change event. This got messy and unreadable very quickly, with thousands of lines being printed out to the console with an integer on each line. This is not very useful, as shown in the following:

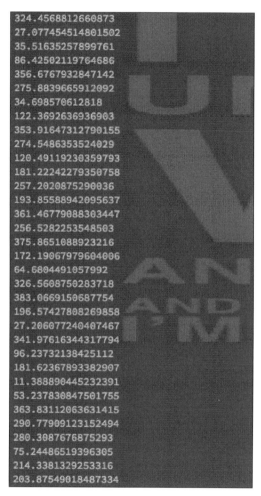

An output in the days before barcli

Luckily, Donovan Buck (who we'll see again in the Animation chapter) wrote a handy Node module called barcli (pronounced BAHRK-LEE) that makes it easy to render bar graphs in the console. This is the best way to show sensor data in the console, because you can see it being updated in real time, and it's much more readable than thousands of lines of integers!

You can find barcli here: `https://github.com/dtex/barcli`. In order to install barcli so that we can use it in the same folder as your code, run the following:

```
> npm install barcli
```

In order to create our graph with the range of our photocell (0 to 1023), we'll use the following code:

```
var barcli = require('barcli');
var graph = new barcli({
  label: 'photocell',
  range: [0, 1023]
});
```

To set the graph, we'll use the following:

```
graph.set([photocell value]);
```

These graphs are much easier to read, as shown in the following example:

A barcli graph in the console

Coding everything together

Using our knowledge of Johnny-Five, the `Sensor` object, and now barcli, we can write the following in `photocell.js`:

```
var five = require('johnny-five');
var Barcli = require('barcli');

var board = new five.Board();
var graph = new Barcli({
  label: 'Photocell',
  range: [0, 1023]
});

board.on('ready', function(){
  var photocell = new five.Sensor('A0');

  photocell.on('data', function(){
    graph.update(this.value);
  });
});
```

Now that we've written the code, run it with the following:

```
> node photocell.js
```

The bar graph in your console should be updated as you cover up or shine a light on the photocell.

Now that we've explored a typical Sensor object, let's take a look at a specialized one using our temperature sensor. We'll write a small application that logs in to bar graphs the temperature detected by the sensor in Fahrenheit, Celsius, and Kelvin.

Wiring up the temperature sensor

Use the following wiring diagram to wire up your TMP36 or LM35 temperature sensor:

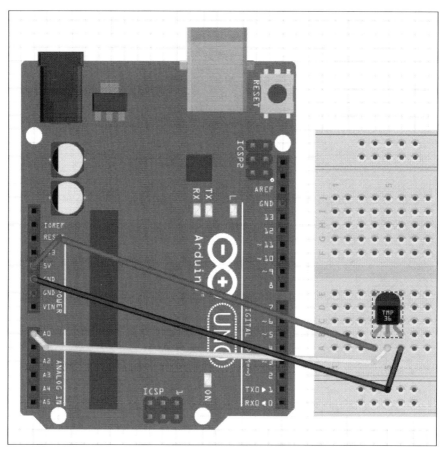

Wiring up the temperature sensor

One way to check that your TMP36 or LM35 is wired correctly is by wiring it up and then plugging the board into your computer. Put your fingers near the temperature sensor. Do they feel warm? Then you have the ground and the power flipped. The diagram assumes the flat side is facing you — remember this, but it's always good to double-check!

Coding our temperature example

Looking at the API for the temperature sensor object, we'll notice that there are no special API calls. However, there are special attributes of the this object inside our data event handler. These attributes allow us to access the Fahrenheit, Celsius, and Kelvin readings for our temperature sensor without doing the translation math ourselves.

With our prior knowledge of Sensor objects and barcli, we can write the following in temperature.js:

```
var five = require('johnny-five');
var Barcli = require('barcli');

var board = new five.Board();

var fahrenheitGraph = new Barcli({
  label: 'Fahrenheit',
  range: [20, 120]
});

var celsiusGraph = new Barcli({
  label: 'Celsius',
  range: [6, 50]
});

var kelvinGraph = new Barcli({
  label: 'Kelvin',
  range: [250, 325]
});

board.on('ready', function(){
  var temp = new five.Temperature('A0');

  temp.on('data', function(err, data){
    fahrenheitGraph.update(data.fahrenheit);
    celsiusGraph.update(data.celsius);
    kelvinGraph.update(data.kelvin);
  });
})
```

Now, we just run this with the following:

```
> node temperature.js
```

We should see three bar graphs in the console as follows:

The temperature.js console output

Try putting something warm or cold near the sensor to see how the bar graph changes!

Summary

In this chapter, we've learned how to use many different input devices and sensors in order to build Johnny-Five projects that listen to the world around them. We've learned how to listen for events, as well as use both the generic `Sensor` object and specialized objects like `Button` and `Temperature`.

In the next chapter, we'll start looking at moving robots using sensors.

6
Moving Your Bot

In this chapter, we will cover the following topics:

- The different kinds of servos and motors
- Special concerns when using motors and servos
- Wiring up servos and motors
- Creating a project with a motor and using the REPL
- Creating a project with a servo and a sensor

What you'll need for this chapter

You'll need your microcontroller—I highly recommend the Arduino Uno for this chapter because of its compatibility. You'll also need your USB cable, a breadboard, some breadboard wires, and a 10k ohm resistor. Grab a photocell, or any other sensor you'd like to try.

You'll also need a motor that runs on 5V and a standard hobby servo that uses 5V. These can be found easily at hobby stores or on Adafruit, SparkFun, Seeed studio, and many other online shops. Check out the following section to see some of your options.

The different kinds of servos and motors

First, we'll go over a few common servos and motors that you'll run into. But first, for those who are new to this, let's look at a quick description of motors and servos.

Defining motors and servos

A motor (or an electrical motor for our purposes) converts electrical energy to motion. Electricity goes in, motion comes out. This motion is output as a rotation motion; one of the most common uses of electronic motors is to turn wheels. Note that while you can control the speed of a motor by controlling the power being input, you cannot change the position of a motor precisely.

This is where servos come in. Servos use electricity to move to a set point—most commonly in an arc of 180 degrees. However, there are some servos that can rotate 360 degrees. We'll discuss these in a moment. Servos are technically specialized motors, and while motors are used to propel projects, servos are used to control them.

Things to keep in mind

There are quite a few servos and motors available for use with your Johnny-Five projects. While we are going to go over many of these, there are a few things to keep in mind when looking at motors to be used.

For instance, be sure to be aware of the voltage and current needed to power the motor or servo; if this is above 5 volts, you'll need to power them with something other than the Arduino's 5V OUT, and if they draw a lot of current but only use 5V, you might consider an external power supply for your Arduino board. Note that additional electric current is supplied whenever you have multiple servos—but the voltage required stays the same; for instance, if you have two servos that require 5V of voltage but 200 mA of electric current, you still only need 5 volts but you will need 400 mA current! Much of this information can be found on the data sheet for the motor or servo you are using.

Types of motors

While we're going to go over a few types of motors here, keep in mind that the functionality of most of these motors is the same; they have an on and off switch, and you can slightly adjust their speed with power adjustments. However, this doesn't rule out the use of motors entirely—there are some interesting uses as well!

Your standard hobby motor looks like a large cylinder with a few wires on one end and a rod on the other end, like the following figure:

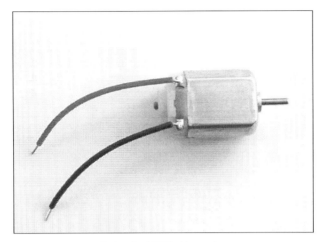

A standard DC hobby motor

The motors come in various sizes and can generate different levels of work. These are mainly used for motion and propelling projects such as remote-control vehicles. Some of these motors are called directional motors—this means you can control the direction. With nondirectional motors, you can only turn the motor in one direction. Keep this in mind when considering your project.

There are also vibration motors—these are found in cell phones that alert you to calls without an audible ring. These look similar to regular motors, but the rod at the end has an asymmetrical weight attached, as shown in the following figure:

A vibration motor

These motors are primarily used for tactile vibration, but in the wearables and cell phone worlds, this can be a vital piece of the puzzle!

Finally, there are stepper motors. They are usually larger and require more power:

A stepper motor

However, stepper motors move in a discreet manner, giving you more control and precision with full rotation. One very common use of these motors is 3D printing—these motors are at the heart of most 3D printers because of their precision and speed.

Types of servos

There are two main types of servos. The first is generally called a standard servo; they are regularly used in hobby remote-control vehicles, such as cars and planes, as well as hobby robotics. These tend to look similar to a box with a plastic cylinder and a propeller, an arm, or a disc shape on top, as shown in the following figure:

A standard servo

These servos move in a range of motion that spans 180 degrees or half of a full range of motion. However, these can be set to a required position giving them precision over motors.

There are also continuous servos that span a full 360 degrees. Note that the two types of servos look remarkably similar; checkout the previous servo and the one shown in the following figure:

A continuous servo

Most continuous servos have a label on them that indicates that they are continuous servos, but you'll have to keep a track of the different types when purchasing your own.

Do I use a servo or a motor?

This is a fantastic question: if you want movement, which one do you use? A servo or a motor? The rule of thumb is, if you want precise movement, you'll need a servo; while servos can be configured to move in certain angles, motors go on and off with the speed setting varied by the amount of power sent to it—not a discrete unit such as degrees/second.

Many of you will think that if you want a full 360 degree range of motors, you're limited to using motors. This isn't always the case; continuous servos combine the precise nature of servos with a full range of motion offered by a motor.

Servo and motor controllers

Sometimes, you may want to use a lot of motors or servos on a project; a good example of this is a hexapod kit, which uses 18 high-powered servos! There are not that many pins on an Arduino Uno, but using a servo or a motor controller, you can control many motors or servos using two data pins. These controllers use the I2C method that we discussed in *Chapter 4, Using Specialized Output Devices*. Johnny-Five has built-in support for quite a few of these controllers. If you'd like to use one, make sure that you check the documentation at www.johnny-five.io to make sure yours is compatible.

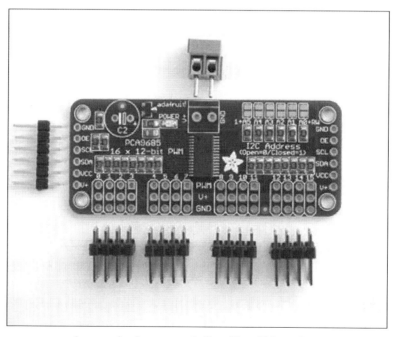

An example of a servo controller with an I2C interface

Motor and servo shields

A shield is an Arduino term for a board that is placed on top of an Arduino, usually an Uno, to give it some extra capability. Shields can be used to add Wi-Fi, LED matrices, and so on. A very common shield type is the shield for motors and servos. Johnny-Five supports a few shields for motor use. Again, if you wish to use a lot of motors or high-powered motors, check out the documentation at `www.johnny-five.io` to see whether a motor shield is right for your project.

An example of a motor shield

Special concerns when using motors and servos

Projects that use servos and motors have some special considerations for them that are mostly focused around power and the fact that Johnny-Five projects are tethered to the computer running the Johnny-Five code.

Power concerns

Servos and motors draw a lot of power. This can be an issue when you are using several of them. If you are using 5V servos and motors and more than two or three at a time, you should use an external power supply for your Arduino to draw this extra current without affecting performance. These power supplies are usually plugged in to an external outlet, and look like the following figure.

WARNING!

Before plugging any external power supply into your board, make sure that the board you are using is voltage regulated for the voltage of the power supply; for an Arduino Uno, this is 12V. When in doubt, use a 5V power supply for Arduinos. Also, follow proper safety protocols when dealing with outside power sources. SparkFun has a great guide at https://learn.sparkfun.com/tutorials/how-to-power-a-project.

If you are using servos or motors that require more than 5V, you will need to supply power externally to your motors or servos. This is outside the scope of this book.

Tethering and cables

Johnny-Five usage means that the code running on the board is receiving messages from the host computer. If this connection is lost, the project cannot run. This means that for most Johnny-Five projects, you will need to maintain a USB cable connection. So if you're going to make a project that involves motion, you'll want a long USB cable.

There are options for wireless NodeBots using Johnny-Five described in *Chapter 9, Connecting NodeBots to the World, and Where to Go Next*.

Wiring up servos and motors

Wiring up servos will look similar to wiring up sensors, except the signal maps to an output. Wiring up a motor is similar to wiring up an LED.

Wiring up servos

To wire up a servo, you'll have to use a setup similar to the following figure:

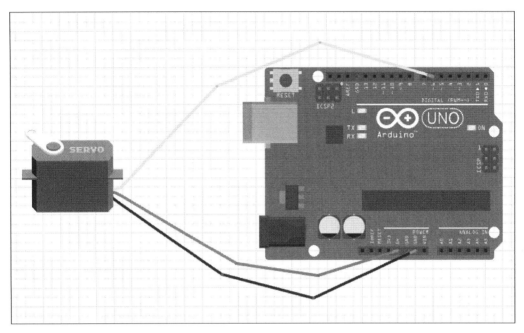

A servo wiring diagram

 The wire colors may vary for your servo. If your wires are red, brown, and orange, red is 5V, brown is **GND**, and orange is signal. When in doubt, check the data sheet that came with your servo.

After wiring up the servo, plug the board in and listen to your servo. If you hear a clicking noise, quickly unplug the board—this means your servo is trying to place itself in a position it cannot reach. Usually, there is a small screw at the bottom of most servos that you can use to calibrate them. Use a small screwdriver to rotate this until it stops clicking when the power is turned on.

This procedure is the same for continuous servos—the diagram does not change much either. Just replace the regular servo with a continuous one and you're good to go.

Wiring up motors

Wiring up motors looks like the following diagram:

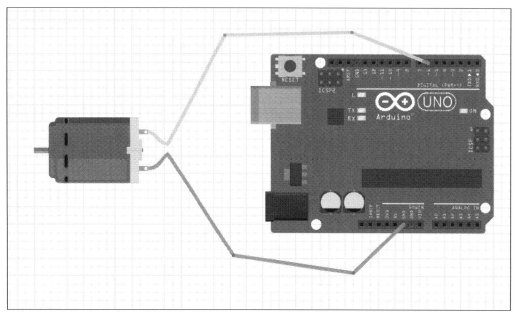

A motor wiring diagram

Again, you'll want the signal pin to go to a PWM pin. As there are only two pins, it can be confusing where the power pin goes—it goes to a PWM pin because, similar to our LED getting its power from the PWM pin in *Chapter 2*, *Working with Johnny-Five*, the same pin will provide the power to run the motor.

Now that we know how to wire these up, let's work on a project involving a motor and Johnny-Five's REPL.

Creating a project with a motor and using the REPL

Grab your motor and board, and follow the diagram in the previous section to wire a motor. Let's use pin 6 for the signal pin, as shown in the preceding diagram.

What we're going to do in our code is create a `Motor` object and inject it into the REPL, so we can play around with it in the command line. Create a `motor.js` file and put in the following code:

```
var five = require('johnny-five');

var board = new five.Board();

board.on('ready', function(){

  var motor = new five.Motor({
    pin: 6
  });

  this.repl.inject({
    motor: motor
  });
});
```

Then, plug in your board and use the `motor.js` node to start the program.

Exploring the motor API

If we take a look at the documentation on the Johnny-Five website, there are a few things we can try here. First, let's turn our motor on at about half speed:

```
> motor.start(125);
```

The `.start()` method takes a value between 0 and 255. Sounds familiar? That's because these are the values we can assign to a PWM pin! Okay, let's tell our motor to coast to a stop:

```
> motor.stop();
```

Note that while this function will cause the motor to coast to a stop, there is a dedicated `.brake()` method. However, this requires a dedicated break pin, which can be made available using shields and certain motors.

If you happen to have a directional motor, you can tell the motor to run in reverse using `.reverse()` with a value between 0 and 255:

```
> motor.reverse(125);
```

This will cause a directional motor to run in reverse at half speed. Note that this requires a shield.

And that's about it. Operating motors isn't difficult and Johnny-Five makes it even easier. Now that we've learned how this operates, let's try a servo.

Creating a project with a servo and a sensor

Let's start with just a servo and the REPL, then we can add in a sensor. Use the diagram from the previous section as a reference to wire up a servo, and use pin 6 for signal.

Before we write our program, let's take a look at some of the options the Servo object constructor gives us. You can set an arbitrary range by passing [min, max] to the range property. This is great for low quality servos that have trouble at very low and very high values.

The type property is also important. We'll be using a standard servo, but you'll need to set this to continuous if you're using a continuous servo. Since standard is the default, we can leave this out for now.

The offset property is important for calibration. If your servo is set too far in one direction, you can change the offset to make sure it can programmatically reach every angle it was meant to. If you hear clicking at very high or low values, try adjusting the offset.

You can invert the direction of the servo with the invert property or initialize the servo at the center with center. Centering the servo helps you to know whether you need to calibrate it. If you center it and the arm isn't centered, try adjusting the offset property.

Now that we've got a good grasp of the constructor, let's write some code. Create a file called servo-repl.js and enter the following code:

```
var five = require('johnny-five');

var board = new five.Board();

board.on('ready', function(){

  var servo = new five.Servo({
    pin: 6
  });

  this.repl.inject({
    servo: servo
  }),
});
```

This code simply constructs a standard servo object for pin 6 and injects it into the REPL.

Then, run it using the following command line:

```
> node servo-repl.js
```

Your servo should jump to its initialization point. Now, let's figure out how to write the code that makes the servo move.

Exploring the servo API with the REPL

The most basic thing we can do with a servo is set it to a specific angle. We do this by calling the .to() function with a degree, as follows:

```
> servo.to(90);
```

This should center the servo. You can also set a time on the .to() function, which can take a certain amount of time:

```
> servo.to(20, 500);
```

This will move the servo from 90 degrees to 20 degrees in over 500 ms.

You can even determine how many steps the servo takes to get to the new angle, as follows:

```
> servo.to(120, 500, 10);
```

This will move the servo to 120 degrees in over 500 ms in 10 discreet steps.

The .to() function is very powerful and will be used in the majority of your Servo objects. However, there are many useful functions. For instance, checking whether a servo is calibrated correctly is easier when you can see all angles quickly. For this, we can use the .sweep() function, as follows:

```
> servo.sweep();
```

This will sweep the servo back and forth between its minimum and maximum values, which are 0 and 180, unless set in the constructor via the range property. You can also specify a range to sweep, as follows:

```
> servo.sweep({ range: [20, 120] });
```

This will sweep the servo from 20 to 120 repeatedly. You can also set the interval property, which will change how long the sweep takes, and a step property, which sets the number of discreet steps taken, as follows:

```
> servo.sweep({ range: [20, 120], interval: 1000, step: 10 });
```

This will cause the servo to sweep from 20 to 120 every second in 10 discreet steps.

You can stop a servo's movement with the `.stop()` method, as follows:

```
> servo.stop();
```

 For continuous servos, you can use `.cw()` and `.ccw()` with a speed between 0 and 255 to move the continuous servo back and forth.

Now that we've seen the `Servo` object API at work, let's hook our servo up to a sensor. In this case, we'll use a photocell. This code is a good example for a few reasons: it shows off Johnny-Five's event API, allows us to use a servo with an event, and gets us used to wiring inputs to outputs using events.

First, let's add a photocell to our project using the following diagram:

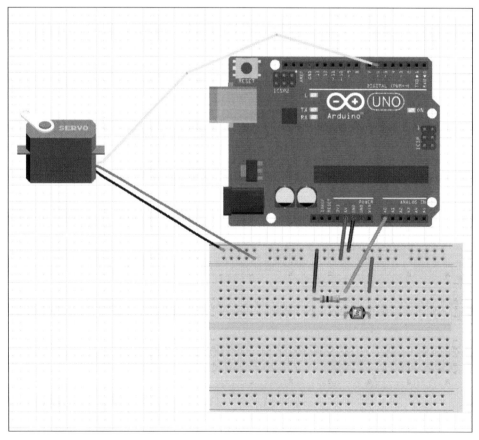

A servo and photoresistor wiring diagram

Then, create a `photoresistor-servo.js` file, and add the following:

```
var five = require('johnny-five');

var board = new five.Board();

board.on('ready', function(){

  var servo = new five.Servo({
    pin: 6
  });

  var photoresistor = new five.Sensor({
    pin: "A0",
    freq: 250

  });

  photoresistor.scale(0, 180).on('change', function(){
    servo.to(this.value);
  });

});
```

How this works is as follows: it's similar to the sensor code we wrote in the previous chapter! It's just during the data event that we tell our servo to move to the correct position based on the scaled data from our photoresistor. Run the following command line:

```
> node photoresistor-servo.js
```

Then, try turning the light on and covering up your photoresistor and watch the servo move!

Summary

We now know how to use servos and motors to move our robotics projects. Wheeled robots are good to go! But what about more complex projects, such as the hexapod? Walking takes timing. As we mentioned in the `.to()` function, we can time servo movement, thanks to the Animation library.

In the next chapter, we'll talk about the Animation library and do some projects that move a few servos in sequence and as a group.

7
Advanced Movement with the Animation Library

Now that we've achieved basic movements in our robotics projects, we're going to explore how to create timed, complex movements. This may seem daunting at first — keeping track of one servo is hard enough! Luckily for us, the Animation library in Johnny-Five makes these complex movements easier to both understand and program. In this chapter, we'll explore what makes the Animation library special and start working with some servo animations. We will cover the following topics:

- What is the Animation API?
- Looking at the Animation API
- Writing servo animations
- Animation events

What you'll need for this chapter

You'll need your microcontroller — I highly recommend the Arduino Uno for this chapter because of its compatibility. You'll also need a USB cable, a breadboard, some breadboarding wires, and the LCD you used in *Chapter 4, Using Specialized Output Devices*. You'll also need three standard servos. If possible, the servos should be of the same brand and make — this will help with our project.

What is the Animation API?

This chapter's title leads to a lot of questions—what is the Animation API and how does it relate to servos? There's also a lot of terminology used here. To start, let's discuss the point and development of the Animation API to give us a little context.

Why do we need an Animation API?

The Animation API was created around the work started by Donovan Buck and Rick Waldron on walking robots—Rick built a quadruped bot, and Donovan, a Hexapod. Turns out, walking robots require a lot of timing on the servos involved, and the Johnny-Five library at the time was only capable of running servos from one degree to another at a maximum speed. This made walking very difficult, because even with servos of the same brand and make, the maximum speed is slightly different. Also, there are situations in which you want different servos to move at different speeds— this was impossible before the Animation API as well.

This led to the development of a function that allows you to set the speed of a given movement by giving a time to complete—we explored these functions in the previous section. You can also set a number of discreet movements. While these definitely helped with walking robotics code, there's another huge benefit to this API, and this is why the name might seem strange.

Why animation?

An animation is a description of movements over time. Keyframes are used in animations to set key positions at given times—there are several animation libraries that will calculate the frames in-between these keyframes, called tweening. The Animation API in Johnny-Five allows you to set keyframes for a servo movement and then does the tweening for you—allowing you to programmatically define a set of movements over time, just as the definition of animation states.

This is great for moving robotics—calculating the speed for each servo in a leg that is moving to a specific point would be daunting for even the most skilled programmer. The Animation API's ability to do tweening for us means that we can set the keyframes and let the code do the rest. This means that even beginners in moving robotics can create complex movements.

Now that we have some context, let's take a bird's-eye view of the Animation API and the various ways to describe and interact with it.

Looking at the Animation API

The Animation API has its own vocabulary — it may be familiar to the readers who have done some animation work. It also has a few different ways to interact with it, and we'll explore these ways before diving in and writing our own projects.

Learning the terminology

There are two parts that make up any servo animation in Johnny-Five: a target and one or more segments. The target is either a servo or an array of servos. We'll go into the programmatic differences between a servo and a servo array in our first project; the basic point is that a `ServoArray` object in Johnny-Five allows a logical grouping and the manipulation of multiple servos — a leg, for instance, would be a logical use of a ServoArray object.

A segment is the programmatic description of a piece of animation. It is comprised of a few pieces of information: a duration, cue points, and keyframes.

A keyframe is a description of the position of the target at a given point. A keyframe has no concept of time; it is an instantaneous description of state. Keyframes are combined with cue points in a segment to add the concept of time.

Cue points are the points at which each keyframe is placed in a segment. This is not a discrete point in time either; cue points are described relative to the segment, usually as a decimal between 0 and 1 where 0 is the beginning of the segment and 1 is the end.

The duration outlines exactly how long the segment will take. The rest of the information uses the duration to calculate the speeds necessary to make it between keyframes at the cue points given. Duration adds the concept of discrete time to a segment.

In order to better understand how these work together, let's walk through a segment description: we have a segment with a duration of 2000 ms (2 seconds). It has cue points at 0, .75, and 1. There are two servos in our target: keyframe 1 has servo 1 at 0 degrees, and servo 2 at 90 degrees. Keyframe 2 has servo one at 45 degrees, and servo 2 at 135 degrees. Keyframe 3 has servo one at 90 degrees, and servo 2 at 180 degrees. So in all, we have a servo starting at 0 degrees and moving to 90 degrees over 2 seconds, and a second servo moving from 90 to 180 degrees in that same 2 seconds.

A graphical representation of this can be seen in the following figure:

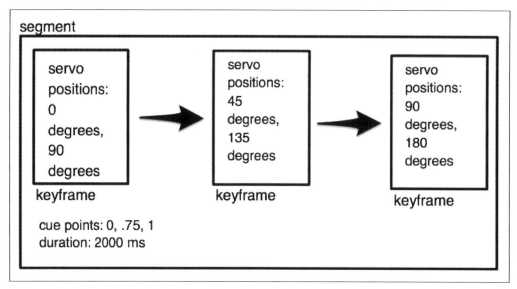

A graphical representation of an animation segment

So, now that we have our segment information, let's use the duration and cue points to see when each keyframe should be reached: the 0 cue point will be reached at 0 ms, the .75 cue point will be reached at 1,500 ms, and the 1 cue point will be reached at 2,000 ms. But how do we determine this? We can use the following formula to determine when a cue point will be reached in a segment:

$$\text{time of cue point} = \text{cue point value} * \text{duration}$$

The formula for a cue point time

So, for the .75 cue point, *2000 ms * .75 = 1500 ms.*

Now, we match these cue points to our keyframes: at 0 ms, servo one will be at 0 and servo two at 90 degrees. At 1500 ms, servo one will be at 45 degrees and servo two will be at 135 degrees, and at 2000 ms, servo one will be at 90 degrees and servo two at 180 degrees. A graphical representation of this is shown in figure 3:

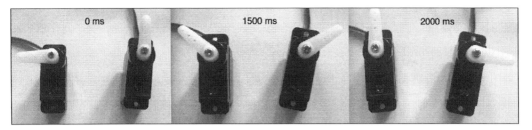

The pictures of the servo movement from the segment

So, in summary, an animation consists of segments applied to a target. Segments consist of keyframes, set to cue points whose timings are determined by the segment's duration.

You get a glimpse of the power the Animation API gives you via this example; trying to calculate the speed needed to move one servo from one degree point to another over *x* milliseconds is a difficult task—to get a lot of servos that represent an arm or leg to do so would be chaotic. The Animation API does this for you by allowing you to set keyframes and cue points in a segment to achieve the movement you want.

The difference between .to() and the Animation API

It may look like the extra options in the `.to()` method for servos allow the creation of animations implicitly. This is not the case!

The `duration` parameter, while allowing servos to move at `nonmax` speeds, does not necessarily serve the same purpose as an animation. The `rate` parameter does not create keyframes; the `rate` parameter creates a number of discrete movements, and they are moved to at the maximum speed.

So, while using `.to()` with durations and rates may seem like creating animations, you should know that they are not a full substitute to write your own animations and segments using the Animation API.

Using the ServoArray object

We've discussed the concept of ServoArray, but let's look at it in a little more detail, as we'll be using it in this chapter's projects.

Constructing the ServoArray object looks remarkably similar to constructing a single servo; however, the object is called `Servos` instead of `Servo`, and you pass in an array of pins representing the pins your group of servos is on:

```
var myServos = five.Servos([3, 5, 6]);
```

This creates an array of servos that are on pins 3, 5, and 6.

Performing actions on a servo array is also remarkably similar to moving a single servo; using `.to()` will move all the servos using the parameters given. For instance, consider the following:

```
myServos.to(120, 500);
```

This will move all the servos in the array to 120 degrees over 500 ms. If you'd like to move one servo independently, all you need is its key in the servo array—you can then reference it and move it as a standard `Servo` object:

```
myServos[0].to(90, 200);
```

This moves the first servo in the array to 90 degrees over 200 ms.

ServoArrays are also very useful in creating animations; you can address an entire array of servos with a single keyframe, allowing you to write keyframes and segments for several servos at once, instead of writing them out separately for each servo.

Now that we've explored the terminology and concepts behind the Animation API, let's build our first project; we're going to build our three servos into a servo array that we can manipulate.

Project – wiring up three servos and creating an array

First, you'll have to wire up your three servos as shown in the following figure:

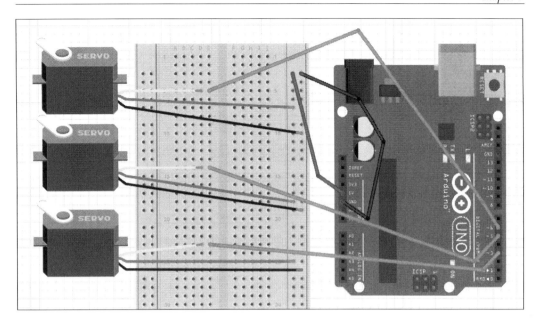

Taking our knowledge of Johnny-Five and the code we went over in the last section, let's write a code to create a servo array of the servos we just wired up and inject them into the REPL so that we can run some code in real time. Place the following into `servo-array.js`:

```
var five = require('johnny-five')

var board = new five.Board({
  port: '/dev/cu.usbmodem14131'
})

board.on('ready', function(){
  var myServos = new five.Servos([3,5,6])
  this.repl.inject({
    servos: myServos
  })
})
```

Now we run it with the following:

```
> node servo-array.js
```

Let it start up. Eventually, the REPL will start and your servos should move to their starting position (the default is 90).

Let's explore moving these servos as a group. Let's sweep them all:

```
>servos.sweep()
```

> If, while sweeping all the servos in your array, they seem choppy, don't fret; we're using three servos now, which takes more electric current than usual. The choppiness is due to a lack of electric current. While this is OK for our present example, you should definitely take a look at the powering servos section in *Chapter 6, Moving Your Bot*, if you want to make a project with multiple servos run smoothly.

We can stop the servos with the following:

```
>servos.stop()
```

Now, let's explore how to use `.to()`, and not only look at how it works with each servo, but also how duration and rate don't substitute the writing of an animation.

We can move all of the servos to the same angle using `.to()`, as follows:

```
>servos.to(0)
```

We can use the same parameters, duration, and rate that we used with a single servo, as shown here:

```
>servos.to(90, 500, 10)
```

That ran pretty smoothly, right? Like an animation would? That's true! But let's slow `.to()` and see what's actually happening here:

```
>servos.to(0)
>servos.to(180, 10000, 20)
```

That's a full 180-degree movement over 10 seconds with 20 discrete steps. Did you notice the choppiness? That's because this writes to `servoWrite()` instead of writing an animation segment.

You can also control one servo at a time as we explored in the last section. For instance, run the following:

```
>servos[0].to(0);
```

This will move the first servo (on pin 3) to 0 degrees, while leaving the other two pins alone.

There are some really great options available in the Animation API that will make these movements smoother and allow you to create complex movements. Let's explore how to declare and run animation segments with Johnny-Five.

Writing Servo Animations

As we discussed in the last section, an animation in Johnny-Five is created and then you enqueue segments that run first-in, first-out. We're going to go from the inside out in our exploration of creating an animation: first, we'll learn about writing keyframes, then segments, and finally we'll explore the Animation object.

Writing keyframes

Writing keyframes are at the core of the Animation API—the power of this API is its ability to tween between our keyframes. Each keyframe is an object, and you'll pass your keyframes into your segment via an array. Remember: you'll want to write a keyframe for each of your cue points.

The keyframe object

As each keyframe is an object, we have access to a few properties that we can establish for each one:

Keyframe	Properties
degrees	degrees is what the name implies; the degree you want the servo to be at when the keyframe is reached. It should be an integer value between 0 and 180 inclusive.
step	step is similar to degrees, but relative to the last keyframe; for instance, if degrees is set to 135 in the first keyframe and step is set to -45 in the next keyframe, the second keyframe will move the servo to 135 - 45 = 90 degrees.
easing	When you create an animation segment, by default any tweening is done at the same speed for the entire span between two keyframes. The easing functions are applied to these frames to change the speed. This can make a motion look more fluid or serve a practical purpose; easing can make quick movements in different directions easier on your servos and equipment.

There are several `easing` functions available via Johnny-Five's use of the `ease-component` module; a very popular one is `inOutCirc`, which causes the frames to move slowly at first, quickly increasing in the middle, and slowing down again towards the end. See the Johnny-Five and `ease-component` docs for more examples of `easing` functions.

Keyframe	Properties
`copyDegrees`	`copyDegrees` calculates the calculated or explicitly set value from the frame at the index given. For instance, let's say we have two keyframes: one has degrees set to `90`, and the second has step set to `45`. If we create a third keyframe with `copyDegrees` set to `0`, it will copy the first frame and set to `90`. If we set the index to `1`, it will copy the second frame and 90 + 45 = 135 degrees will be the setting for the third keyframe.
`copyFrame`	`copyFrame` is similar to `copyDegrees`, but it copies all the attributes of the given frame instead of just the degrees; this includes `easing` functions and so on.
`position`	`position` is an advanced and newer concept in Johnny-Five's Animation API. This allows you to give three tuples that represent a 3D coordinate in space, and it will move the array of servos to this point.
	It is worth noting here that you need more than just Johnny-Five for this to work; you'll need an **IK (Inverse Kinematic)** solver, such as **Donovan Buck's tharp project**. Going into the details of position is outside the scope of this book, as it is still being actively developed and the functionality might change. However, if you're looking to build a robot that moves with you, check this out.

Keyframe shorthand

You can also define keyframes without using objects; if you pass your keyframes as an array of integer values, each integer value will be interpreted as a step value. Consider the following array:

```
keyFrames: [0, 90, -45, 90, -90]
```

This will (assuming a `0` start point) move the servo to 0, 90, 45, 135, and 45 degrees for each cue point.

You can also use non-integer values in shorthand syntax to mean specialized values:

Values	Properties
null	When `null` is passed into a shorthand keyframes array, its value depends on its position. If it is the first keyframe, the segment will use the existing servo position as its first keyframe. If it is last in the array, it will copy the previous keyframe's value.
	However, if it is used between two frames, something interesting happens: it will drop the keyframe, and tweening will be calculated between the keyframe before and after the `null` value. This can be handy if you'd like a servo to take more time between two keyframes.
false	`false`, used anywhere in a shorthand keyframe array, will copy the last known value. It will not move the servo between the two keyframes.

So, in closing, you can use either a keyframe object, a number, `null`, or `false` to represent a keyframe in a segment definition. Now that we've explored the attributes available on a keyframe object, let's write some keyframes to match certain situations.

Examples of writing keyframes

Let's explore some examples of keyframes:

Example 1: Write a set of keyframes that starts a servo at the last position it was at, moves to it by 90 degrees with an `inOutCirc` easing, then moves it by 45 degrees back with no easing:

1. The first keyframe can be handled using the `null` value:

    ```
    var myFrames = [null];
    ```

2. The second requires a keyframe object because we want to establish an `easing` function:

    ```
    var myFrames = [null, { degrees: 90, easing: 'inOutCirc' }];
    ```

3. The last could be done with a keyframe object:

    ```
    var myFrames = [null, { degrees: 90, easing: 'inOutCirc' }, {
    step: -45 }];
    ```

However, we can also use shorthand—remember that passing a number as a keyframe will lead to using that number as a `step` value:

```
var myFrames = [null, {degrees: 90, easing: 'inOutCirc' }, -45];
```

Among the preceding alternatives, which one you use is entirely up to your own preference.

Example 2: Write a set of keyframes that starts the servo at 0, moves to 90, spends two cue points moving to 180, and then moves to 135:

1. The first and second keyframes can be set via a keyframe object, as follows:

    ```
    var myFrames = [{degrees: 0}, {degrees: 90}];
    ```

2. Otherwise for the second keyframe, we can use a shorthand, as shown here:

    ```
    var myFrames = [{degrees: 0}, 90];
    ```

As we know that the first keyframe will set the servo to 0, we can use `step` instead of `degrees`. For the next step, we want the servo to take two cue points to move to 180. We could calculate how to do this with standard keyframes, or we could use a shorthand `null` to tell the segment to skip that cue point and tween between 90 and 180 over two cue points:

```
var myFrames = [{degrees: 0}, 90, null, {degrees: 180}]
```

Now that you've learned how to write keyframe arrays and objects, let's take a look at writing the rest of our Animation object.

Writing segments

We know that segments consist of an array of keyframes, an array of cue points, a duration, and some options. Let's take a look at the options available to us in each segment, and then build some segments to get us ready for our next project.

Segment options

The segment options and their properties are as follows:

Segment options	Properties
target	You can use this in the segment to override the target this segment operates on; this is usually specified by the animation, so setting it in the segment overrides the animation's assignment.
easing	Just like keyframes, you can set an `easing` function for an entire segment. Note that easing functions stack; if you use an easing function on keyframes and a segment, the tweening will calculate the keyframe easing and then the segment easing.

Segment options	Properties
loop	This is a Boolean; true causes this segment to loop when enqueued until it is stopped by the animation it was queued to.
loopBack	If you'd like a looping segment to loop back to some place other than the first cue point, you can specify the index of that cue point here. For instance if a segment has the cue points [0, .25, .75, 1] and you set loopBack to 1, the segment will loop the cue points [.25, .75, 1] only.
metronomic	This is a Boolean; if true, the segment will run from the first cue point to the last, then back to the first in reverse order. You can combine this with the loop option, but it will not loop by default.
progress	This attribute can be either used as information about a running segment (as we'll see in a later project) or set; you can set the current progress of the animation if you'd like to start at a different point. This should be a value between 0 and 1, much like cue points.
currentSpeed	Much like progress, this can be used as information and set. The default is 1.0, and this changes the speed multiplier at which the segment runs.
fps	This sets the maximum frames per second that a segment can run at. The default is 60. Changing the maximum fps of a segment will not change the speed or cue points.

Multiple servos in one segment

More often than not, you'll be animating more than one servo at a time. How do you handle keyframes for more than one servo? By passing an array of arrays; each array represents the keyframes for a servo in the target servo array. For instance, the following segment contains the keyframes for two servos in an array:

```
var myMultiServoSegment = {
  duration: 2000,
  cuePoints: [0, .5, 1],
  keyFrames: [
    [{degrees: 135}, -45, -45]
    [{degrees: 45], 45, 45]
  ]
}
```

Examples of writing segments

Let's walk through a couple of examples of writing segments.

Example 1: Write a sweeping segment that goes from 0 to 180 and back. Give it the inOutCirc easing and make it loop. The duration should be 5 seconds, with as few keyframes as possible.

Now, we could write our keyframes to go from 0 to 180 and back, or we could use the metronomic option to help us out. Using the metronomic function also means that we only need two keyframes and cue points—0 and 1! We'll also need the easing option and the loop option. Here's the result of this example:

```
var sweepingSegment = {
    duration: 5000,
    metronomic: true,
    loop: true,
    easing: 'inOutCirc',
    cuePoints: [0, 1],
    keyFrames: [{degrees: 0}, {degrees: 180}]
}
```

Example 2: Write a segment that runs once. This segment contains instructions for two servos. Servo one starts at whatever position the servo is already at, then adds 45 degrees over 1 second, then removes 30 degrees over 2 seconds, and finally adds 15 degrees over 1 second. The second servo simply moves from 20 degrees to 120 degrees over the duration, with full tweening and the inOutCirc easing. The duration of the segment should be 4 seconds.

We're using relative positions here, so it looks like the keyframes shorthand will come in handy. We have to set unequal cue points at: 0/4, 1/4, 3/4, and 4/4, that is at .25, .75, and 1. Remember— in a keyframe shorthand, null at the beginning means use the current position of the servo, and null in the middle means skip the cue point and recalculate tweening!

Keeping all of this in mind, we get the following:

```
var mySegment = {
    duration: 4000,
    cuePoints: [0, .25, .75, 1] ,
    keyFrames: [
        [null, 45, -30, 15],
        [{degrees: 20}, null, null, {degrees: 120}]
    ]
}
```

This is the true power of the Animation API—we can describe complex movements in objects that mathematically work out.

Now that we know how to write keyframes and segments, let's take a look at writing Animation objects and running segments using them.

The Animation object

The analogy that I like to use for the Animation object is to think of it like an MP3 player. You load tracks into it, and you can press play, pause, or stop. You queue segments into an animation in any order, and you can play, pause, or stop the animation at any time.

Let's take a quick look at the constructor: it only takes one parameter, which is the target. As we mentioned earlier, the target is the servo or an array of servos being animated. So, let's take a look at a sample program that constructs a servo array and constructs an Animation object:

```
var five = require('johnny-five')

var board = new five.Board()

board.on('ready', function(){
  var servos = new five.Servos([3, 5, 6])
  var animation = new five.Animation(servos)
})
```

Once we've constructed the Animation object, the next important function is .enqueue(). You pass a segment to this function to add it to the animation queue. Animations are run first-in, first-out, so our code becomes this:

```
var five = require('johnny-five')

var board = new five.Board()

board.on('ready', function(){
  var servos = new five.Servos([3, 5, 6])
  var animation = new five.Animation(servos)

  var mySegment = {
    easing: 'inOutCirc',
    duration: 3000,
    cuePoints: [0, .25, .75, 1]
    keyframes: [{degrees: 45}, 45, 45, -45]
  }
```

```
    animation.enqueue(mySegment)
})
```

That's the whole kit and caboodle; animations are set to run as soon as a segment is enqued! Let's take an in-depth look at the functions available to the Animation object:

Functions	Properties
.enqueue()	.enqueue() places a segment in the queue for the animation. Segments are run first-in, first-out when an animation is played.
.play()	.play() plays the animation, starting with the first segment put in that hasn't already been run. It will also continue the last segment in progress if the animation was paused.
.pause()	.pause() stops the animation, but maintains progress on any in-progress segments and maintains the segment queue.
.stop()	.stop() clears the segment queue as well as stops all animation.
.next()	.next() clears the current segment and moves on to the next. However, this is not automatically called by the animation when each segment finishes and is normally not called by the user.
.speed([speed])	.speed() can be used to view (when no arguments are passed) or set (when a number representing a multiplier is passed) the speed of the current animation.

Now that we know how animations work in general, let's build our own project with our three servos. Let's animate!

Project – animating our servo array

You should still have your servo array from the last project. Let's animate it! We'll use the REPL to modify our animation segment in real time and play with some of the true power of the Animation API.

Let's start with the code that initializes our board, sets up our servo array, creates an animation and a segment, and inserts them into the REPL. Place the following into animation-project.js:

```
var five = require('johnny-five')

var board = new five.Board()

board.on('ready', function(){
  var servos = new five.Servos([3, 5, 6])
  var animation = new five.Animation(servos)

  var mySegment = {
    easing: 'inOutCirc',
    duration: 3000,
    cuePoints: [0, .25, .75, 1],
    keyFrames: [
      [{degrees: 45}, 45, 45, -45],
      [{degrees: 30}, 30, 30, 30],
      [{degrees: 20}, 40, 40, 40]
    ]
  }

  this.repl.inject({
    animation,
    mySegment
  })

  animation.enqueue(mySegment)
})
```

Go ahead and run this with the following:

```
node animation-project.js
```

Your servos should spring to life and should start running the segment (we queued it on the last line!). Once it's done running, let's see it again on a loop. In the REPL, type the following:

```
>mySegment.loop = true
>animation.enqueue(mySegment)
```

The segment should start running on a loop. Want to see it slower? Let's change the speed using the Animation object's speed() function:

```
>animation.speed(.5)
```

This should slow it down to half speed. Let's go ahead and stop the animation, clearing the queue:

```
>animation.stop()
```

Let's see what happens when we make our segment `metronomic` using an `easing` function, and then run it:

```
>mySegment.easing = 'inOutCirc'
>mySegment.metronomic = true
>animation.enqueue(mySegment)
```

The segment now loops forward and reverses and looks more fluid!

This is cool, but what if we want animations to run one after the other? We could use a series of durations and timers, or we could tap into Johnny-Five's event system, which extends through the Animation API. Next we'll explore how to tap into these events to create timed animations.

Animation events

A lot of movements require waiting for one segment to finish before starting another. Some segments should only be fired at certain times, as well. The best way to handle these timings and communication systems is by using Johnny-Five's `animation` events.

We tap into these events by assigning callbacks to special attributes on segments. Let's go into the details of each one and see when they will fire.

Events	Details
onstart	The `onstart` callback fires when the segment has begun playing in the animation.
onstop	The `onstop` callback is only called when the segment is either in the queue or currently running, but the animation is stopped via `animation.stop()`.
onpause	The `onpause` callback is only called when the segment is queued or running in an animation that has been paused via `animation.pause()`.

Events	Details
oncomplete	The oncomplete callback only fires when the segment has completed running in an animation. Note: This does *NOT* apply to looped segments. See the onloop callback for this.
onloop	The onloop callback is called when a function loops, that is at the beginning of the second run-through and each started run-through thereafter.

In order to understand how the events work and what they can be used for, let's start on our final project: grab your LCD from *Chapter 4, Using Specialized Output Devices,* and your servo array from earlier in the chapter, and let's build.

Building a servo array with an informative LCD readout

Using the following diagrams, build your project; the first diagram is for I2C LCD displays:

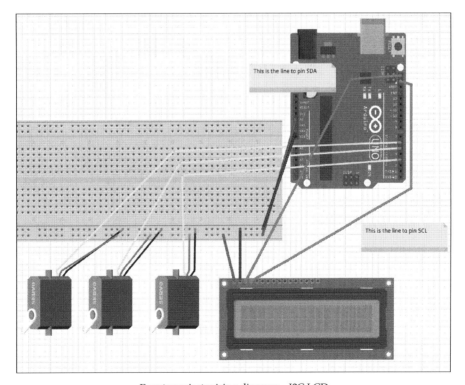

Events project wiring diagram — I2C LCD

The second diagram is for standard LCD displays:

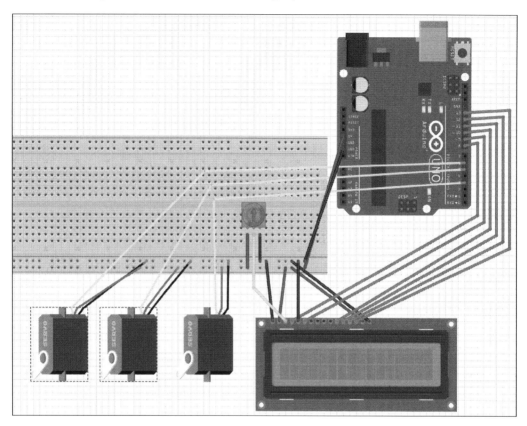

Events project wiring diagram—Standard LCD

Once you've wired it up, you'll notice that we can modify the last piece of code we wrote to include our LCD and create functions for each event. Let's add the following to our segment: a callback for each event type that prints to the LCD `segment [event name]!`.

When you've added the LCD code and the event callbacks, your code should look like this. Let's create a new file called `animation-events.js` for this:

```
var five = require('johnny-five')

var board = new five.Board()
board.on('ready', function(){
  var servos = new five.Servos([3, 5, 6])
  var animation = new five.Animation(servos)
  //For I2CLCDs, uncomment these lines:
  // var lcd = new five.LCD({
```

```
//   controller: 'PCF8574A'
// })
//NOTE: for standard LCDs, uncomment these lines:
// var lcd = new five.LCD({
  // pins: [8, 9, 10, 11, 12, 13]
// })

var mySegment = {
  easing: 'inOutCirc',
  duration: 3000,
  cuePoints: [0, .25, .75, 1],
  keyFrames: [
    [{degrees: 45}, 45, 45, -45],
    [{degrees: 30}, 30, 30, 30],
    [{degrees: 20}, 40, 40, 40]
  ],
  onstart: function(){
    lcd.clear()
    lcd.print('Segment started!')
  },
  onpause: function(){
    lcd.clear()
    lcd.print('Segment paused!')
  },
  onstop: function(){
    lcd.clear()
    lcd.print('Segment stopped!')
  },
  onloop: function(){
    lcd.clear()
    lcd.print('Segment looped!')
  },
  oncomplete: function(){
    lcd.clear()
    lcd.print('Segment completed!')
  }
}

this.repl.inject({
  lcd,
  animation,
  mySegment
})

animation.enqueue(mySegment)
})
```

Let's try this out! Go ahead and run this with the following:

```
node events-project.js
```

You should see **Segment started!** as soon as the program starts—this is because we enqueue the segment right away. Once it's done, you should see **Segment Complete!**.

To test `onloop`, `onpause`, and `onstop`, let's modify our segment to run on a loop and enqueue it:

```
>mySegment.loop = true
>animation.enqueue(mySegment)
```

You should see the `start` event, then if you let it run for a bit, it'll show **Segment looped!**.

Now let's pause it to see the `pause` event:

```
>animation.pause()
```

You should see **Segment paused!**. Let's re-run it, then stop to see the `onstop` event:

```
>animation.play()
>animation.stop()
```

You should see **Segment stopped!**.

Summary

You now know just about everything there is to know about the Animation API as it applies to a servo movement. More functionality is being added to the Animation API to work with other devices, such as LEDs—so keep an eye on `johnny-five.io` to see more!

In the next chapter, we'll look at adding other devices to your Johnny-Five projects, such as other USB devices and complex components.

8

Advanced Components – SPI, I2C, and Other Devices

We've covered a lot of different types of device already—including input, output, and movement. This chapter delves into how these devices can be implemented in different ways and for different reasons. In this chapter, we'll take a look at the I2C and SPI protocols and their advantages and setbacks with Johnny-Five. We'll also take a look at how to add your own components to Johnny-Five, which gives us a good look into how these devices work and how you can contribute to the development of Johnny-Five! In this chapter, we will cover the following topics:

- Why do we need the I2C and SPI protocols?
- The SPI devices
- The I2C devices
- External devices

What you'll need for this chapter

You'll need your microcontroller, a USB cable, and computer. You'll also need an ADXL345I2C Accelerometer such as the Adafruit Industries product ID 1231 or the SparkFun product ID SEN-09836, and an LED matrix kit from SparkFun— product number DEV-11861. You'll also need your LCD display from *Chapter 4, Using Specialized Output Devices*. Finally, you'll need a USB gamepad—I recommend the N64RetroLink controller that is available for about $15 on Amazon, but if you have a spare PS3DualShock 3 controller, I will also include instructions for that.

Why do we need the I2C and SPI protocols?

This is all starting to get really complicated, right? Why even bother? We have digital pins and analog pins; shouldn't reading values from these be enough?

Not when you go outside the realm of LEDs. Think about how much information goes into this text you're reading on a page (or, likely, a screen)! Bytes and bytes of information. This is true for many peripherals you'll use in Johnny-Five applications.

For instance, the accelerometer we'll be using—without the I2C protocol, it would use three analog pins. That's the majority of the analog pins on an Arduino Uno, and many platforms don't have analog pins at all! Not to mention the LCD we used in *Chapter 4*, *Using Specialized Output Devices*—without I2C, we have to correctly wire 11 different pins, six of which are separate data pins.

The complexity of data being sent and received is also an issue. There are sensors that send back data that doesn't fit in an analog range of 0-1024. There are output devices—such as LCD screens—that need bytes of information. These devices need these protocols to effectively communicate and receive the data they need.

The I2C and SPI protocols allow us to unlock an entirely new dimension of data for small projects—we can use many more devices with way fewer pins.

First, we'll take a look at the SPI protocol—this protocol allows us to send a lot of data in a much easier way than previous setups.

Exploring SPI (Serial Peripheral Interface) devices

Serial Peripheral Interface (**SPI**) is a protocol to be used with certain devices in Johnny-Five and in general, robotics. It came about as a response to typical serial connections (which you don't see often in hobbyist robotics anymore), which were asynchronous in nature. This led to a lot of overhead, so SPI was developed as a way to ensure data was sent and received in a way that was efficient.

Keep in mind that when we talk about synchronous/asynchronous in this context, we are *NOT* talking about it as we would in JavaScript. You can still write async JavaScript functions around SPI methods!

How SPI works

In typical serial connections, you have a line from which data goes out (TX) and a line to which the data comes in (RX), and this makes communication difficult. How does the receiver know how fast the sender would be sending bytes, and when are they done sending? This lack of a synchronized time clock is what we mean when we say asynchronous in this context—the sending and receiving devices just send bytes as fast as they please, assuming the receiver will know how to read them.

Let's go through some of the features of SPI:

- SPI uses a separate pin to establish a unified time clock, to sync the receiver and sender. This data clock is flipped between a HIGH and LOW state each time a bit is sent—telling the receiver that a new piece of information is being read.

- SPI also splits the communications lines into **MOSI (Master Out Slave In)** and **MISO (Master In Slave Out)**. I'll refer to these by their acronyms, but I will use microcontrollers and devices for our purposes, as in this context they work well.

- The MOSI pin is the line to send data from the microcontroller to the device—output, for our purposes. MISO is a line for the device to send data to the microcontroller—great for sensors and other input needs. Note that if a device does not have any reason to communicate data back to the microcontroller (like our LED matrix), it may leave off the MOSI pin and label the MISO pin something such as "data".

- Finally, SPI devices usually have a **CS** or **SS** pin (**Chip Select** or **Slave Select**), which is used in setups where multiple devices are used by one microcontroller. This pin is flipped between HIGH and LOW to let the microcontroller tell the device that it is sending data. You flip the CS pin of the device you are reading from or writing to, and other devices will ignore that data.

So to recap, you need four pins on average—one for the synchronous clock (often labeled SCLK), one for the microcontroller to send data to the device, one for the device to send data to the microcontroller, and one for chip selection.

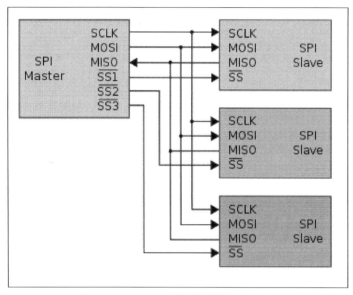

The SPI explained—Image credit: `https://en.wikipedia.org/wiki/Serial_Peripheral_Interface_Bus`

 Note that in many setups with one SPI device, wiring diagrams will show that the CS pin is wired to the 5V. This is fine—you're just permanently setting the CS to HIGH, telling the device to always be listening for or sending data.

How Johnny-Five does SPI

Luckily, we don't have to handle timing and bit-shifting ourselves—Johnny-Five gives us a nice API to deal with SPI connections. The functions for these are attached to the Board object and are usually accessed by the component libraries themselves—you won't be using these much unless you're implementing your own SPI device!

This method handles the sending out of data to the device. Also, this is the method used for our LED matrix. The method, Board.shiftout(dataPin, clockPin, data), shifts out the bytes in data through the pin dataPin using clockPin as a clock.

So considering what we know of SPI, we can determine that Johnny-Five does the following for us:

1. Sets the clock, data, and CS pins to the OUTPUT mode.

2. Sends startup instructions specific to our device (in the case of our LED matrix, brightness and refresh rate are two examples).

3. Waits for data to be sent by our program.

4. Sets the CS pin to LOW to indicate to our device that data is being sent to it.

5. Writes the data and syncs the clock and data pins for us.

6. Sets the CS pin back to HIGH to indicate we are done sending data.

Benefits and drawbacks of SPI

The benefits of SPI are mainly in the speed and ease-of-use categories; it's way easier to write to and read from SPI devices because they agree on timing and you don't need extra bits or patterns to alert devices of the beginning and end of data.

The downside involves the sheer number of pins required; whereas serial connections only required two pins, SPI requires four, with only one pin that can be shared with multiple SPI devices. Your SPI devices can all share a clock pin, but need their own MISO, MOSI, and CS pins. This can proliferate quite quickly.

Luckily, Johnny-Five has SPI support on quite a few platforms, most notably Arduino microcontrollers. Next, we'll take a look at building a project with an SPI device—our LED matrix!

Building with an SPI device – an LED matrix

For our first project, we're going to use an SPI device with our Arduino and Johnny-Five. What we'll use is an LED matrix. This is a matrix of several single-, dual-, or tri-color LEDs that are controlled as a group.

You can really see the benefit of SPI here—controlling each of these LEDs with a pin would require 64 pins for a single-color matrix! For dual- and tri-color, it would be 128 and 192! SPI really gives us a boost here by allowing us to have control based on two pins.

The build

Grab your LED matrix and wire it up! Here's the pin matchup in case you have a different LED matrix: pin 2 runs to DIN or DATA, pin 3 to SCLK, CLK, or clock, and pin 4 to CS, as shown in the following diagram:

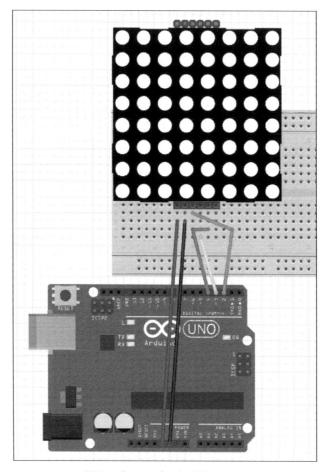

Wiring diagram for the LED matrix

Note that the item in the diagram has one extra pin— ignore that! Yours should only have five, and the pins should be clearly labeled on any kit you get.

The API

The LED matrix API in Johnny-Five gives us a lot of ways to play with this output device. Let's take a look at the constructor and a few of the methods, in the following table, before breaking into our code:

 Note that in the API, many of these functions take an optional index—this is because you can chain LED matrices together and this optional parameter allows you to address each one specifically. We won't be using this here because we only have one device.

Methods	Properties
.on([index])	This turns on all the matrices if no index is passed. It turns off the device at an index if an index value is passed.
.off([index])	This turns off all the matrices if no index is passed, and the one at an index if it is passed. Note that when a matrix is turned off, it still retains data that will be shown when the matrix is turned back on—this can be used as a power saver for battery-run projects!
.clear([index])	This clears all matrices if no index is passed, and clears the matrix at an index if one is passed. This clears out the data and turns all LEDs in the matrix off.
.brightness([index], brightness)	If no index is passed, this sets all matrices to the brightness passed (0-100). If an index is passed, this sets the matrix at that index to the passed brightness level.
.led([index], row, col, state)	If no index is passed, this sets all matrices at the point (row, col) to state (1 for ON, 0 for OFF). If an index is passed, this sets only the LED on that matrix.

There are also functions to draw multiple LEDs at once, but we'll need to talk a bit about how we pass drawing data to the LED matrix first.

Formatting data for the LED matrix

As you can see from the preceding `.led()` function, 1 sets the LED to ON and 0 sets it to OFF. This is a lot like binary, right? That's because it is, and that's how we send all data to the LED matrix—a series of binary bits.

So, for instance, you can send an image to an LED matrix that's 8x8 with an array of rows represented by strings containing binary values for each LED in the row:

```
var checkerboard = [
    "01010101",
    "10101010",
    "01010101",
    "10101010",
    "01010101",
    "10101010",
    "01010101",
    "10101010"
];
```

However, this can get unwieldy. You can also send the same data as a set of hexadecimal values representing each row, with two digits in each number; our first row in binary is 0b01010101, which translates to 0x55, and our second row in binary is 10101010, which translates to 0xAA:

```
var checkerboardHex = [0x55, 0xAA, 0x55, 0xAA, 0x55, 0xAA, 0x55, 0xAA];
```

Keep these in mind as we talk about the next set of functions, which I call the drawing functions.

The Drawing functions

Let's explore some of the drawing functions in the following table:

Functions	Properties
`.row([index], row, value);`	If an index isn't passed, this sets the LEDs in a row at `row` to `value`—where the value is an 8-bit or 16-bit value (0-255 in decimal). If an index is passed, this only sets the row at that device's index.
`.column([index], col, value),`	If an index isn't passed, this sets the LEDs in the column at `col` to `value`—where the value is an 8-bit or 16-bit value (0-255 in decimal). If an index is passed, this only sets the row at that device's index.

Functions	Properties
`.draw([index], character);`	This draws a character on the device at an index, if passed. If no index is passed, this renders the character on all devices.

So, `.row()` and `.column()` work with one hexadecimal value— `.row(0, 0xFF)` sets the first row of LEDs to ON for all matrices.

`.draw` can accept a few things as a valid input. We have shown many of these in previous examples: Strings of binary characters and hexadecimal values, both in an array of rows. But luckily, the library already has several characters implemented for us. The predefined characters for LED matrices in Johnny-Five are as follows:

- 0 1 2 3 4 5 6 7 8 9...
- ! " # $ % & ' ( ) * + , - . / : ; < = > ? @
- A B C D E F G H I J K L M N O P Q R S T U V W X Y Z [\ ] ^ _ `
- a b c d e f g h i j k l m n o p q r s t u v w x y z { | } ~

You can pass in a string containing one of these characters as your value, as shown here:

```
myMatrix.draw('~');
myMatrix.draw('A');
```

This allows us much more easily to show text and numerical output on our LED matrix.

Now that we've explored the API, let's write some code that loads a character that we define, then injects our matrix and another character that we define into the REPL so we can play with it live!

The Code

Place the following into `led-matrix.js`:

```
var five = require("johnny-five");
var board = new five.Board();

board.on("ready", function() {

  // our first defined character-- using string maps
  var checkerboard1 = [
    "01010101",
    "10101010",
```

```
        "01010101",
        "10101010",
        "01010101",
        "10101010",
        "01010101",
        "10101010"
    ];

    //our second defined character-- using hex values
    var checkerboard2 = [ 0xAA, 0x55, 0xAA, 0x55, 0xAA, 0x55, 0xAA,
    0x55];

    var matrix = new five.Led.Matrix({
    pins: {
    data: 2,
    clock: 3,
    cs: 4
      }
    });

    matrix.on();
    matrix.draw(checkerboard1); //draw our first character

    this.repl.inject({
      matrix: matrix,
      check1: checkerboard1,
      check2: checkerboard2
    });
});
```

Once you've got the code in, run it with the following:

```
node led-matrix.js
```

In a few seconds, your LED matrix should light up with a checkerboard pattern like the following:

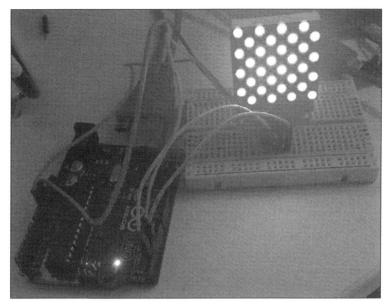

A matrix example with checkbox character

Now's the time to play with the REPL—for instance, try the following command line:

```
matrix.draw(check2);
```

And watch it change! You can also clear the matrix with the following command line:

```
matrix.clear()
```

Draw a predefined character with the following command line:

```
matrix.draw('J');
```

After clearing again, try the .led and .row functions as follows:

```
matrix.clear();
matrix.led(3, 3, 1)
matrix.row(1, 0xA1);
```

You now have a good grasp of the LED matrix and using SPI devices with Johnny-Five! We've discussed the upsides and downsides of SPI communications and covered a little about why serial connections remove and create a lot of overhead. Now, we're going to take a look at I2C—a protocol designed to gather many of the benefits of SPI and serial and join them together.

Exploring I2C devices

We touched on I2C devices back in *Chapter 4, Using Specialized Output Devices* — you may have used an I2C LCD to display some data. You may have noticed that the I2C LCD was much easier to wire up, and had the same API as the non-I2C LCD. Luckily, this is because Johnny-Five strives to give every component a similar API, regardless of its implementation or protocol. But how does I2C work, and what makes it a useful protocol?

How I2C works

I2C, which stands for Inter-Integrated Circuit, is a protocol that input and output components can use to communicate with microcontrollers. It's very standardized, and nearly all I2C devices operate in the same way. I2C also has the major benefit of being recognized and implemented by many major microcontroller manufacturers — including Arduino. Any Arduino platform that is compatible with Johnny-Five is also compatible with I2C devices.

However, implementing an I2C device in Johnny-Five can be a tricky proposition. To understand why, we need a better understanding of how I2C works.

I2C has the good parts of SPI combined with the good parts of serial communications. It only uses two pins for data and clock, but has a synchronous clock that can be set by the system!

Pins used by I2C

I2C devices use two pins outside of any power requirements: SDA, which is a data line, and SCL, which is a clock line. These two pins form an information bus, which can be used by many devices at once.

This is where it sounds a lot like SPI; the two pins drive each other. When sending an instruction, the SCL pin is flipped, telling the bus that another bit of data is ready, while simultaneously flipping the SDA bit to the value of the bit being sent. This allows the programmer and microcontroller to dynamically control the clock — this allows accurate data transmission and very few bit errors. However, it can be very difficult to implement this behavior ourselves.

Each time data is sent to I2C, an address is sent as the first byte. This address refers to the device on which our microcontroller is.

Luckily, we don't have to implement this behavior ourselves—Johnny-Five and the underlying Firmata system have implemented this for us. However, you will need to understand how to write and read from these devices—otherwise, you'll be stuck with a device that won't even boot up!

How I2C devices send and receive data

Every I2C device has an address, which is usually shown in hexadecimal format. For instance, the address of the accelerometer that we'll be using in this chapter is `0x53` (the `0x`, for those unfamiliar with hexadecimal, indicates that the number is in hexadecimal format). This is useful when the I2C bus for a microcontroller is controlling multiple devices—the address tells the devices on the bus which device we are writing to or reading from. An example of address use can be as follows:

Data is sent and received by writing to and reading from registers on the I2C device. Every time we want to write to or read from an I2C device, we need to send the address (so the devices on the bus know which device you are addressing to) and the register we want to read or write. If we are writing data, we also need to send the byte we wish to write.

Benefits and drawbacks of I2C

There are definitely benefits and drawbacks of using I2C with Johnny-Five, and they can affect your builds or choice of microcontroller.

Benefits

Let's go through the benefits of using the I2C devices, as follows:

1. One of the benefits of using I2C devices is that you can use several devices with just two data pins: SDA and SCL. As this is built on a bus, you can use several devices without any issues.

2. Another benefit of I2C devices is that they conform to a standard; implementing these standards mostly conforms to a formula that is easier to follow than the devices with a less rigid standard (or no standard!).

3. Finally, there are many I2C backpacks for devices that use several data pins otherwise—such as our LCD from earlier. These backpacks can make devices useable with microcontrollers using fewer pins. There is even some work being done in Johnny-Five to use I2C expanders, which will allow devices without analog input or PWM pins to use devices that require these pins. This is called the Expander API and more info can be found on this at `johnny-five.io`.

Drawbacks

Let's go through the drawbacks of using the I2C devices, as follows:

1. One of the main drawbacks of using I2C in Johnny-Five is that not all platforms that run Johnny-Five support it—be sure to check the **Platform Support** section of `johnny-five.io` before trying I2C with your device.

2. Another drawback of implementing new I2C devices is that timing can be an issue—I2C is very synchronous by nature; it requires certain instructions to be sent in a certain order with certain delays in between. Johnny-Five and JavaScript are not the easiest to wrap around these concepts, and this can cause some really interesting race conditions and bugs. However, these issues only appear when implementing your own I2C devices.

Building with an I2C device – Accelerometer

Building a Johnny-Five project with an I2C component can sound tricky—luckily, because of the way Johnny-Five works, it's actually nearly as simple as other projects we've worked on in this book. For this project, you'll need your microcontroller, your breadboard and wires, and your ADXL345 accelerometer.

Wiring up our accelerometer

To get started, wire up your project as shown in the following diagram. Be sure that you only use the I2C pins and the power pins on your accelerometer. Also, be sure to use as many jumper wires as you can, as you have been able to move the breadboard and the accelerometer around a bit to test this project:

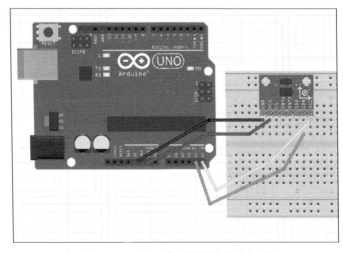

Accelerometer wiring for NON-R3 Arduino Uno

One last thing to note: if you use the SparkFunADXL345 board, you'll need to wire the CS (Chip Select) pin to VCC, as shown here:

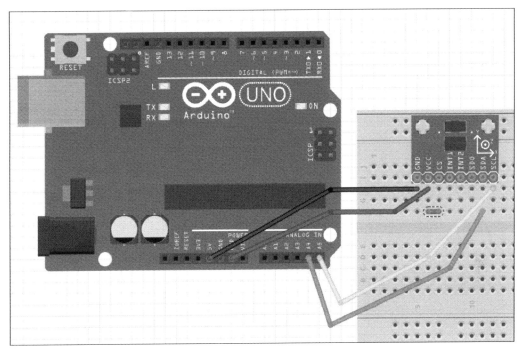

Wiring for the SparkFun breakout board

You do *NOT* need to do this for the AdafruitADXL345 board.

Once you've wired the accelerometer up, it's time to write the code to test that everything works. We'll be using `barcli` again, to show each axis of acceleration easily.

Coding up our example

In order to code our example, we should first look at the `Accelerometer` object and API to see which events to watch for.

Looking at the API, we'll want to tap into the `change` event. Luckily for us, we can also tap into a lot of information regarding the accelerometer, thanks to the Johnny-Five API. Inside the `change` event handler, we can access the following bits of data:

Data	Properties
`this.x`	This is the value for the *x* axis in G forces
`this.y`	This is the value for the *y* axis in G forces

Data	Properties
`this.z`	This is the value for the z axis in G forces
`this.pitch`	This is the pitch of the device in degrees
`this.roll`	This is the roll of the device in degrees
`this.acceleration`	This is the total acceleration of the device
`this.inclination`	This is the inclination (incline measure) of the device
`this.orientation`	This is a value between -3 and 3 representing the physical orientation of the device

Since we want to show bar graphs of the output, let's consider the ranges we'll need to set on these graphs. The axes' raw data doesn't tell us too much, so let's skip the graphs of these. pitch, roll, and inclination are in degrees, so we'll set the range from -180 to 180. And acceleration will be between -2 and 2g, although you can set this higher for the ADXL345—up to 16g. Orientation will be between -3 and 3.

Knowing all of this, we can write our code as follows:

```
var five = require('johnny-five');
var barcli = require('barcli');
var board = new five.Board();

board.on('ready', function(){
  //set up our accelerometer
  var accel = new five.Accelerometer({
    controller: 'ADXL345'
  });

  //set up our graphs
  var pitch = new barcli({
    label: 'Pitch',
    range: [-180, 180]
  });
  var roll = new barcli({
    label: 'Roll',
    range: [-180, 180]
  });
  var acceleration = new barcli({
    label: 'Acceleration',
    range: [-2, 2]
  });
  var inclination = new barcli({
```

```
    label: 'Inclination',
    range: [-180, 180]
  });
  var orientation = new barcli({
    label: 'Orientation',
    range: [-3, 3]
  });

  accel.on('change', function(){
    pitch.update(this.pitch);
    roll.update(this.roll);
    acceleration.update(this.acceleration);
    inclination.update(this.inclination);
    orientation.update(this.orientation);
  });
});
```

Once you've got all this in, place your accelerometer so that it is laid flat on a table, and start up the program with the following:

`node accel-i2c.js`

You should see your terminal clear, and several bar graphs appear, like the figure below:

Barcli bar graphs in the terminal

As you move the accelerometer, watch the values change! The bar graphs should, as always, update live in the terminal.

There are many projects you can continue within this vein—you can attach servos to match pitch and roll angles, or LEDs to get brighter when you accelerate! You can achieve a lot of input from your accelerometer that can influence and add extra dimensions to your NodeBots projects.

Now that we've gone through the two most popular protocols to communicate with the devices connected to our microcontrollers, let's explore the world beyond a bit—let's talk about using external devices in your Johnny-Five projects.

External Devices

SPI, I2C, and some other protocols get really complex, but there's a whole other world of devices we can also use with our Johnny-Five projects. These technically fall outside the scope of the Johnny-Five library, but works well with the library due to their use of Node.JS. Let's take a look at the "why" and the "how" of external devices with Johnny-Five.

Why External Devices?

Microcontrollers are amazing! They can do a litany of things—input, output, and so on - but sometimes you see a new device that doesn't plug in to a microcontroller. Perhaps it contains a microcontroller of its own—such as a quadcopter or a drone! This section covers the use of these devices with Node and integrating them into your Johnny-Five projects.

Some really cool examples that have been integrated into Johnny-Five projects are as follows: video game controllers; the `LeapMotion` controller, a gesture sensor that tracks hand position and movement; and Wi-Fi-enabled quadcopters, such as the Parrot AR drones.

But how do we communicate with devices without using Johnny-Five? The answer actually lies within Johnny-Five itself: `node-serialport`, a library that handles serial connections via Node.JS. Let's take a look at how this library enables us to build the amazing world of NodeBots.

node-serialport

As early as five years ago, NodeBots didn't exist. As early as ten years ago, they weren't even a thought—JavaScript was a browser language, after all. However, with the advent of Node, all sorts of new technologies were available to Node.

Serial connections are the communications channel between all sorts of devices— such as printers, webcams—and many of the peripherals that we use on a daily basis. In 2009, Chris Williams (often cited as the Godfather of NodeBots!) created `node-serialport`. The `node-serialport` library allows you to communicate with serial devices using Node.JS.

At first, this didn't create the explosion of NodeBots you'd expect by reading a book like this—it was still a very specialized thing to get a serial connection working. However, shortly after the creation of `node-serialport`, Rick Waldron wrote Johnny-Five on top of it. That's right; under its hood, Johnny-Five uses `node-serialport` to speak to the Arduino boards we've been using in our examples.

However, there are other devices that have made their way to Node using libraries outside `node-serialport`; these include gamepads meant for playing games on the PC. Many devices that you can add to your computer via USB can now be used with Node, thanks to another library called `node-hid`.

node-hid

The `node-hid` library is for using **Human Interface Device (HID)** devices, such as gamepads. HID is a part of the USB specification and allows many peripherals to speak to a computer in a way that is easily understood and emulated.

Some of the most popular HID devices used are gamepads, computer games, and retro system emulators. In our next build, we'll explore how to use these external devices with Johnny-Five, using a library called `node-gamepad`.

Building a USB gamepad

What we're going to build is a hybrid project; we'll be using Johnny-Five along with other Node plugins in order to expand the reach of things we can do. We're going to show the x and y coordinates from the joystick on the N64RetroLink controller (or left on the PS3 controller) on our LCD display.

The hardware

First, let's wire our LCD to our Arduino to show data on. Remember to use the first diagram for I2C displays and the second for regular LCD displays:

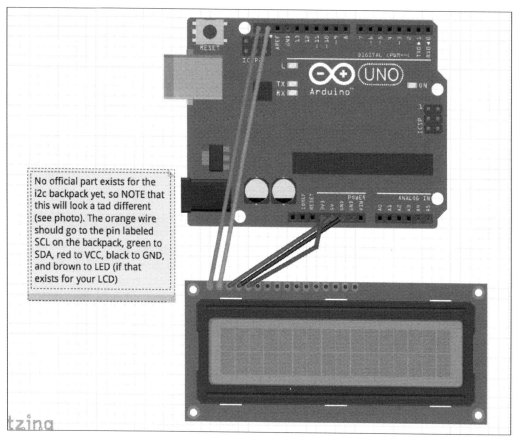

No official part exists for the i2c backpack yet, so NOTE that this will look a tad different (see photo). The orange wire should go to the pin labeled SCL on the backpack, green to SDA, red to VCC, black to GND, and brown to LED (if that exists for your LCD)

Wiring diagram—I2C LCD

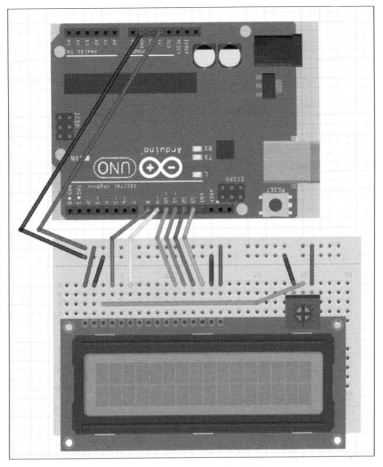

Wiring diagram—regular LCD

Once you've wired up your LCD, connect your gamepad to your computer. If you're using the RetroLinkN64 controller, plug it in via USB. If you're using the PS3 controller, you can pair it with Bluetooth or connect it via USB.

The node-gamepad API

Let's take a look at the `node-gamepad` library before writing our code. First, let's install the library:

```
npm install node-gamepad
```

This will install the library and rebuild the native bindings for `node-hid`. Then, let's take a look at the gamepad constructor:

```
var GamePad = require('node-gamepad');
var gamepad = new GamePad('n64/retrolink'); //using PS3? use 'ps3/
dualshock3' instead
```

The constructor just takes a path to a keymap provided by the library; use n64/retrolink for the retrolink controller and ps3/dualshock3 for the PS3 controller.

For the joystick data, we'll need to put an event handler on the joystick so that we get a response when it moves:

```
gamepad.on('center:move', function(data){ … }); //Using PS3? use
'left:move'
```

The data object will have an x and a y property, representing the x and y coordinates of the joystick.

Now that you know what to look for from the gamepad, you can wire this code together with your existing Johnny-Five knowledge!

The code

Create a `controller.js` file and add the following lines of code:

```
var five = require("johnny-five");
var GamePad = require( 'node-gamepad' );
var board = new five.Board();

var controller = new GamePad( 'ps3/dualshock3' );
controller.connect();

board.on("ready", function() {
  // Controller: PCF8574A (Generic I2C)
  // Locate the controller chip model number on the chip itself.
  var l = new five.LCD({
    controller: "PCF8574A",
  });
```

```
//If you're using a regular LCD, comment the previous three
// lines and uncomment these lines:
// var l = new five.LCD({
//   pins: [8, 9, 10, 11, 12, 13]
// });

var x, y;

// if you're using a PS3 controller, change center:move to
//   left: move!
controller.on( 'center:move', function(data) {
  x = data.x;
  y = data.y;
});

// Updates on an interval to not overwhelm the LCD!
setInterval(function(){
  l.clear();
  l.cursor(0, 0).print('X: ' + x);
  l.cursor(1, 0).print('Y: ' + y);
}, 250)
});
```

Start the file using the following command line:

`node controller.js`

You should see the LCD update when you move the joystick!

Now here's a challenge; add a listener for one of the controller buttons to show on the LCD as well!

Summary

We've done a lot in this chapter. You've learned about SPI, I2C, and how to use external libraries and devices with Johnny-Five. In the next (and sadly, final) chapter, we'll discuss the use of different microcontrollers with Johnny-Five and how to connect your projects to the Internet.

9
Connecting NodeBots to the World, and Where to Go Next

We have now covered just about everything you need to break into the wide world of JavaScript Robotics—except how to connect your bots to the web, and where to go from here. This chapter covers how to connect your NodeBots to online services, such as Twilio, and how Johnny-Five and other libraries will lead you to exploring your next set of projects!

In this chapter, we will cover the following topics:

- Connecting NodeBots to the Web
- Johnny-Five and the wide world of microcontrollers
- Other JS Robotics libraries and platforms
- Where to go from here

What you'll need for this chapter

You'll need your microcontroller, a temperature sensor, and a button—we're going to build a bot that sends a text message with the inside and outside temperature data when you press the button. If you can get your hands on a Particle Photon (check out the shop at `www.particle.io`), you'll also learn how to make your code work on both platforms without changing more than two lines!

Finally, you'll need your enthusiasm and curiosity—these are the things that'll give you ideas for your next NodeBots project!

Connecting NodeBots to the Web

Bots are really cool on their own—collecting data, outputting that data using colors, text, and even images! We can only do so much when our bots only talk to themselves. However, because of the Node platform that we build our NodeBots on, talking to web services and using Internet data in our projects is really simple. How so? Well, all you have to remember about NodeBots code is the following.

It's just a Node Server!

Implementing data retrieval and third-party APIs in our NodeBots is easy—especially when, thanks to npm, the modules that interface with all our favorite APIs are right at our fingertips.

Anything that you can install on your computer from npm, you can use with your NodeBots. For instance, I have a wearable that pulls colors from tweets—I use Twitter and the color modules from npm to make this happen smoothly!

For our first example, we're going to build a relatively simple bot, hardware-wise. It'll have a button and a temperature sensor. However, we're going to connect this bot to the Internet and have it collect weather data and use Twilio to text us this data.

Using Twilio

In order to get started, you'll have to follow the instructions at `http://twilio.github.io/twilio-node/` to get your own account, phone number, and API keys. Once you've done this, you'll need to save the keys and phone number for use in our project code.

Building the WeatherBot

First, let's wire up the WeatherBot, as shown in the following diagram:

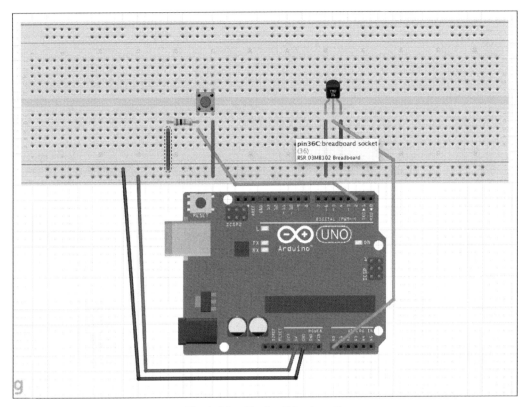

The Arduino WeatherBot schematic

Once you've wired it all together and got your Twilio API keys and phone number, it's time to start coding.

Let's take a look at the steps that we need to take:

1. We need to establish our weather and Twilio services, create our board, and start the board.

2. Then, when the board is ready, we need to create a temperature sensor and a `button` object.

3. When the temperature sensor updates, we need to update a variable with the current indoor temperature.

4. When the button is pressed, we need to go get the outside weather data, and combining this with our indoor weather data, we have to send a text message using our new Twilio client.

So we'll need the following in a file called `arduino-weatherbot.js`:

```javascript
var five = require('johnny-five');
// we'll use weather-js for the weather
var weather = require('weather-js');
// and Twilio so send our text message
var twilio = require('twilio')(YOUR_ACCOUNT_SID, YOUR_AUTH_TOKEN)

var board = new five.Board();

board.on('ready', function(){
  var button = new five.Button(2);
  var temp = new five.Temperature({
    pin: 'A0',
    controller: 'TMP36' // Make sure you use the controller proper
      for your sensor!
  });

  var currentTemp = undefined; // we'll stash the temp sensor data
here

  button.on('press', function(){
    console.log('Inside: ' + currentTemp + ' degrees F');
    weather.find({ search: 'Austin, TX', degreeType: 'F' },
      function(err, data){
      console.log('Outside: ' + data[0].current.temperature + '
        degrees F');
      twilio.sendMessage({
          to: YOUR_PHONE_NUMBER,
          from: YOUR_TWILIO_NUMBER,
          body: 'Inside: ' + currentTemp + ' degrees F \n Outside:
            ' + data[0].current.temperature + ' degrees F'
      }, function(err, responseData) {
        if(!err){
          console.log('Success!');
        } else {
          cosole.log(err); // we need to catch any Twilio errors
        }
      });
    })
  })

  temp.on('change', function(err, data){
    currentTemp = data.F; //stash the temp data when it changes!
  });
});
```

Once you've got all this, keep in mind what you need to change: YOUR_ACCOUNT_SID and YOUR_AUTH_TOKEN need to be replaced with the keys you received from the Twilio API, YOUR_PHONE_NUMBER needs to be replaced with a number you can text, and YOUR_TWILIO_NUMBER needs to be replaced with the number you received from Twilio. Finally, you should change Austin, TX to your location for more accurate data!

Using the TextBot

Now, grab your cell phone and run the code:

```
node arduino-weatherbot.js
```

Once you've pressed the button, wait a bit, and you should see a text message in your phone's inbox!

The text message from my WeatherBot!

You've now connected your NodeBots to two online services: weather-js uses Yahoo weather and Twilio!

We've done a lot with our Arduino Uno, and it's been great, but let's talk about moving on to other microcontrollers and how easy this can be with Johnny-Five!

Johnny-Five and the wide world of microcontrollers

We've been using Johnny-Five for the majority of this book, but we haven't really touched on one of its best features! While the REPL and the API are definitely strong points, what really stands out about it is its wide array of supported microcontrollers.

To be up to date with what Johnny-Five supports, check out johnny-five.io/platform-support—this page, as we saw in the earlier chapters, contains all the platforms that Johnny-Five supports, and also what types of component they support.

Wrappers, which we'll use in this build, are pieces of code that translate Johnny-Five's Firmata method of communicating to other platforms that don't necessarily use Firmata. In our build, for instance, we'll be using a Particle Photon, which uses a firmware called **VoodooSpark**. The `particle-io` wrapper essentially teaches Johnny-Five how to speak VoodooSpark, so we can use the Photon with our existing code.

Let's check out how easy it is to move code by moving our Arduino Uno WeatherBot to the Particle Photon, a Wi-Fi-connected microcontroller that is available at **particle. io**. There are definitely some differences between our Uno and the Photon: the Photon is a $20, Wi-Fi-connected device, and it comes with free cloud services provided by Particle.

Once you've received your Photon, you have to use `particle-cl` to create an account and claim your Photon. Do this by plugging your Photon into a USB port, and while the status light flashes blue, install the CLI using npm and run the setup:

```
npm install -g particle-cli
particle setup
```

Once you've run the setup, you'll need your access token and device ID. To get the device ID, run the following:

```
particle list
```

Then, copy the hex identifier for the Photon you just set up. To get your access token, run the following:

```
particle token list
```

Next, copy the hex value for any nonexpired token.

Finally, we need to flash our Photon with VoodooSpark, a firmware that, like Firmata on the Uno, allows our Johnny-Five code to communicate with our Photon. You can go about this in two ways: one is to follow the instructions at `https://github.com/voodootikigod/voodoospark`, and the other is to use the new command-line tool, `voodoospark-installer`. To use the new CLI, install it as follows:

```
npm install -g voodoospark-installer
```

Then, run the following:

```
voodoospark
```

This will ask for your Particle username and password, and then give you a list of Photons to pick from. Select your new Photon, hit *Enter*, and it will install VoodooSpark on that Photon.

Moving our WeatherBot to the Particle Photon

First, let's look at the hardware setup for this bot. It's very similar to the Arduino Uno build, but the pins are a bit different:

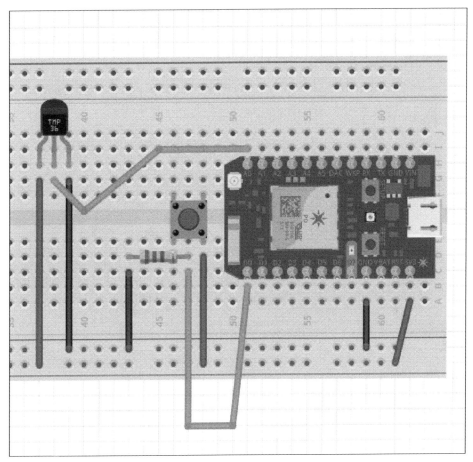

A WeatherBot Photon schematic

Next, we'll need to enter our project folder and install `particle-io`. The `particle-io` module is a Johnny-Five wrapper module—it tells Johnny-Five how to communicate with the Photon, because it is slightly different to communicating with the Arduino.

```
npm install particle-io
```

Now, we need to add the wrapper to our code. I suggest that you copy your original code to a new file called `photon-weatherbot.js`:

```javascript
var five = require('johnny-five');
// our particle-io wrapper
var Particle = require('particle-io');
// we'll use weather-js for the weather
var weather = require('weather-js');
// and Twilio so send our text message
var twilio = require('twilio')(YOUR_ACCOUNT_SID, YOUR_AUTH_TOKEN)

var board = new Particle({
  deviceId: YOUR_DEVICE_ID,
  token: YOUR_ACCESS_TOKEN
});

board.on('ready', function(){
  var button = new five.Button('D0');
  var temp = new five.Temperature({
    pin: 'A0',
    controller: 'TMP36' // Make sure you use the controller proper for
your sensor!
  });

  var currentTemp = undefined; // we'll stash the temp sensor data
here

  button.on('press', function(){
    console.log('Inside: ' + currentTemp + ' degrees F');
    weather.find({ search: 'Austin, TX', degreeType: 'F' },
function(err, data){
      console.log('Outside: ' + data[0].current.temperature + '
degrees F');
      twilio.sendMessage({
        to: YOUR_PHONE_NUMBER,
        from: YOUR_TWILIO_NUMBER,
        body: 'Inside: ' + currentTemp + ' degrees F \n Outside: ' +
          data[0].current.temperature + ' degrees F'
      }, function(err, responseData) {
        if(!err){
          console.log('Sucess!');
        } else {
          cosole.log(err); // we need to catch any Twilio errors
        }
```

```
      });
    })
  })

  temp.on('change', function(err, data){
    currentTemp = data.F; //stash the temp data when it changes!
  });
});
```

Note the changes; we need to require in our wrapper, place it in our `Board` object constructor, and change the pins for the button and temperature sensor.

That's it! The rest of the code will work the same, and this is true for *ANY* platform that Johnny-Five supports. This is one of the biggest strengths of Johnny-Five; we have an ubiquitous API to build NodeBots on tons of different platforms with very little code change. Run this, and watch it work!

Now that we've explored how to change platforms, let's look at why changing platforms can be beneficial, depending on the type of project you are working on.

Tethering and Johnny-Five

You may have noticed one limitation of our Arduino setup with Johnny-Five: we have to keep our microcontroller attached to our computer via USB and keep the Node code running on the computer in order to keep Johnny-Five running. Luckily, this isn't the case for all NodeBots on Johnny-Five. For instance, the BeagleBone Black runs Node on-board, and so, using `beaglebone-s`, you don't need to tether. You just run the Johnny-Five code straight on the device. This is also true for `raspi-io` for Raspberry Pi and `tessel-io` for the Tessel 2.

More and more devices will be added to Johnny-Five as time goes on, and tethering limitations will become less and less of an issue accordingly.

Other JS libraries and platforms

Johnny-Five is definitely an amazing library and one of the cornerstones of NodeBots. However, one of the great things about open source hardware and software is that there is a litany of choices for you to explore in the world of NodeBots. I'll go into just a few of the many available, as new choices and projects are popping up every day!

Espruino

Espruino is an open source effort by Gordon Williams to create a microcontroller that runs JavaScript right on the board. There are currently two models available: the Espruino, which is the size of a credit card, and the Pico, which is nearly stamp-sized. Both interact via a USB connection.

Note that the Espruino doesn't use Node; it uses its own version of JavaScript that is in some places heavily modified. However, to most JavaScript developers, it will feel remarkably familiar.

The Espruino uses a Chrome app to code and flash the board, and has a good amount of documentation. As the entire effort is open-source, users are welcome to contribute. You can find out more about the Espruino at `www.espruino.com`, and the boards are available for purchase on Adafruit.

Tessel

The Tessel project is another fully open sourced platform that has two versions. Tessel 1 ran a Node-like environment using a LUA interpreter under the hood, and Tessel 2 runs Linux with Node on top. Note that the Johnny-Five wrapper `tessel-io` only works for Tessel 2! However, both of these boards are very interesting and fairly easy to use without Johnny-Five, and are well-supported and documented by the Tessel steering committee.

Tessel 2 was ready to be shipped soon at the time of writing this book, and you can check out its progress or pre-order/buy one at `tessel.io`.

Cylon.js

Cylon.js is a library much like Johnny-Five, which also supports many platforms. Its focus is also slightly broader. While Johnny-Five sticks to making sure that microcontroller support is the main focus, Cylon supports other serial peripherals. You can find out more about this open-source project at `cylonjs.com`.

JerryScript

JerryScript is a brand new open-source project from Samsung to get a JavaScript engine running in a small enough amount of memory so that it can run on a microcontroller without Linux running underneath. While this is a very new and ambitious project, if it succeeds, it can usher in a whole new era of JavaScript robotics. You can learn more at `https://samsung.github.io/jerryscript/`.

Tiny Linux computers

While this is less of a concerted effort and more of a category of devices, there are new, smaller, faster Linux machines coming out every few months. From Raspberry Pi to Onion Omega, these machines that carry their own GPIO are definitely an interesting segment of devices to explore. Many have their own GPIO Node modules outside of Johnny-Five. BeagleBone Black has BoneScript, for instance. Keep an eye out in the future for more of these tiny computers, and definitely consider them for your standalone NodeBots projects.

Vendor libraries

Many IoT microcontrollers also come with JS libraries to use. For instance, Particle has released an npm module to work with their Core and Photon platforms over their cloud service using the Spark package. (Note that, because of their company name change, this package name may change when this book is published). Many vendors are moving to support Node on their own terms, so definitely look for an npm package when looking at new hardware platforms.

Where to go from here

As we near the end of this book, I'll address the questions that I get most often: Where do I go from here? What do I build? Who do I ask for help?

As for what to build, you can do as I do. I keep a small notebook with me, although I also use my phone to record thoughts—I think about the small things I'd like to have in my day-to-day life. What problems can I solve? What would look cool? I write down these problems or wants and go over them later. Can I fix this with a NodeBot, I ask myself. If I can, awesome! I have my next project. I think you'll find you have more ideas than you thought you did with this method.

Once you've built something, write about it! The NodeBots community loves to see how you built something. Don't worry if it's not the next terrain-navigating hexapod; we'd like to see how you built your Internet-connected Christmas lights or your automatic dog-feeder. You can never have too many examples for people to look at, and one of the best ways to contribute back is documentation.

What if you get a new part working? Submit a pull request to Johnny-Five. The team is very good about issuing fast and friendly feedback, and will work with you to get your component into Johnny-Five. Also, come and say "Hi" in our Gitter channel— we're super friendly and love to meet new users and NodeBotters.

Thanks for taking this journey through JavaScript Robotics with me! I'm `nodebotanist` on Twitter, GitHub, and just about anywhere—come and say "HI" and show me what you've built!

Index

C

character LCD
  code, running 40, 41
  code, writing 39
  connecting, to Arduino Uno board 35
  I2C LCDs, wiring 35-38
  I2C version, coding 39
  non-I2C version, coding 39
  without I2C interface, URL 30
Chip Select (CS) 99
Cylon.js
  about 130
  URL 130

D

**development environment,
    for JavaScript robotics**
  Firmata, installing 4-6
  Johnny-Five, installing 3
  microcontroller, connecting 4-6
  Node.js, installing 3
  project, setting up 3
digital output pins
  and PWM pins, differentiating
    between 20, 21
Donovan Buck's tharp project 84
drawbacks
  of I2C device 110
  of SPI device 101

E

Espruino
  about 130
  URL 130
events, Johnny-Five program
  about 11
  importance 11
external devices
  about 114
  importance 114
  node-hid library 115

node-serialport library 114, 115
USB gamepad, building 115
external LED
  hardware, setting up 12-14
  importance 12
  wiring 12

F

Firmata
  installing 4
functions, Johnny-Five program 10

G

**General-Purpose Input/Output pins
    (GPIO pins)**
  digital output pins 20
  PWM output pins 20
  working 19, 20
GitHub
  URL 35

H

Hello, World!
  onboard LED, blinking 7
Human Interface Device (HID) devices 115

I

I2C devices
  benefits 109
  data, receiving 109
  data, sending 109
  drawbacks 109, 110
  exploring 108
  pins 108, 109
  used, for building accelerometer 110
  working 108
I2C protocol
  need for 98
inject method 15
Inter-Integrated Circuits (I2C) 32
Inverse Kinematic (IK) 84

Thank you for buying
Learning Javascript Robotics

About Packt Publishing

Packt, pronounced 'packed', published its first book, *Mastering phpMyAdmin for Effective MySQL Management*, in April 2004, and subsequently continued to specialize in publishing highly focused books on specific technologies and solutions.

Our books and publications share the experiences of your fellow IT professionals in adapting and customizing today's systems, applications, and frameworks. Our solution-based books give you the knowledge and power to customize the software and technologies you're using to get the job done. Packt books are more specific and less general than the IT books you have seen in the past. Our unique business model allows us to bring you more focused information, giving you more of what you need to know, and less of what you don't.

Packt is a modern yet unique publishing company that focuses on producing quality, cutting-edge books for communities of developers, administrators, and newbies alike. For more information, please visit our website at www.packtpub.com.

About Packt Open Source

In 2010, Packt launched two new brands, Packt Open Source and Packt Enterprise, in order to continue its focus on specialization. This book is part of the Packt Open Source brand, home to books published on software built around open source licenses, and offering information to anybody from advanced developers to budding web designers. The Open Source brand also runs Packt's Open Source Royalty Scheme, by which Packt gives a royalty to each open source project about whose software a book is sold.

Writing for Packt

We welcome all inquiries from people who are interested in authoring. Book proposals should be sent to author@packtpub.com. If your book idea is still at an early stage and you would like to discuss it first before writing a formal book proposal, then please contact us; one of our commissioning editors will get in touch with you.

We're not just looking for published authors; if you have strong technical skills but no writing experience, our experienced editors can help you develop a writing career, or simply get some additional reward for your expertise.

Arduino Robotic Projects

ISBN: 978-1-78398-982-9   Paperback: 240 pages

Build awesome and complex robots with the power of Arduino

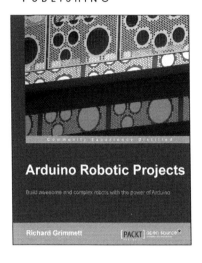

1. Develop a series of exciting robots that can sail, go under water, and fly.

2. Simple, easy-to-understand instructions to program Arduino.

3. Effectively control the movements of all types of motors using Arduino.

4. Use sensors, GPS, and a magnetic compass to give your robot direction and make it lifelike.

Arduino Development Cookbook

ISBN: 978-1-78398-294-3   Paperback: 246 pages

Over 50 hands-on recipes to quickly build and understand Arduino projects, from the simplest to the most extraordinary

1. Get quick, clear guidance on all the principle aspects of integration with the Arduino.

2. Learn the tools and components needed to build engaging electronics with the Arduino.

3. Make the most of your board through practical tips and tricks.

Please check **www.PacktPub.com** for information on our titles

BeagleBone Robotic Projects

ISBN: 978-1-78355-932-9   Paperback: 244 pages

Create complex and exciting robotic projects with the BeagleBone Black

1. Get to grips with robotic systems.

2. Communicate with your robot and teach it to detect and respond to its environment.

3. Develop walking, rolling, swimming, and flying robots.

Arduino Home Automation Projects

ISBN: 978-1-78398-606-4   Paperback: 132 pages

Automate your home using the powerful Arduino platform

1. Interface home automation components with Arduino.

2. Automate your projects to communicate wirelessly using XBee, Bluetooth and WiFi.

3. Build seven exciting, instruction-based home automation projects with Arduino in no time.

Please check **www.PacktPub.com** for information on our titles

27348020R00091

Made in the USA
San Bernardino, CA
11 December 2015